PENGUIN MODERN MASTERS

EDWARD EVANS-PRITCHARD

Mary Douglas received her Ph.D. from Oxford
University, where she studied under Edward
Evans-Pritchard, in 1951. She was a member of
the faculty of University College London until
1977 and is the author of five books and numerous articles. Dr. Douglas is currently working at
the Russell Sage Foundation in New York City.

Frank Kermode, King Edward VII Professor of
English Literature at Cambridge University, is
the author of *The Classic; D. H. Lawrence;
Shakespeare, Spenser, Donne;* and other widely
acclaimed critical studies.

MODERN MASTERS

ALREADY PUBLISHED

PENGUIN
MODERN MASTERS

EDITED BY frank kermode

*By Modern Masters we mean the men who
have changed and are changing the life and
thought of our age. The authors of these
volumes are themselves masters, and they
have written their books in the belief that
general discussion of their subjects will
henceforth be more informed and more exciting than ever before.* —F. K.

edward evans-pritchard

mary douglas

PENGUIN BOOKS

Penguin Books Ltd, Harmondsworth,
Middlesex, England
Penguin Books, 625 Madison Avenue,
New York, New York 10022, U.S.A.
Penguin Books Australia Ltd, Ringwood,
Victoria, Australia
Penguin Books Canada Limited, 2801 John Street,
Markham, Ontario, Canada L3R 1B4
Penguin Books (N.Z.) Ltd, 182–190 Wairau Road,
Auckland 10, New Zealand

First published in the United States of America by
The Viking Press 1980
Published in Penguin Books 1981

LIBRARY OF CONGRESS CATALOGING IN PUBLICATION DATA
Douglas, Mary Tew.
Edward Evans-Pritchard.
Bibliography: p.
Includes index.
1. Evans-Pritchard, E. E. (Edward Evans),
1902–1973.   2. Ethnology—Great Britain.
I. Title.
GN21.E93D68   1981   301′.092′4   81-11844
ISBN 0 14 00.5927 X   AACR2

Printed in the United States of America by
Kingsport Press, Inc., Kingsport, Tennessee
Set in Primer

Grateful acknowledgment is made to Oxford University
Press for permission to reprint selections from *Nuer
Religion* by Edward Evans-Pritchard (1956) and
The Nuer by Edward Evans-Pritchard (1940).

CONTENTS

ACKNOWLEDGMENTS

I thank the Russell Sage Foundation, New York, in whose employ I am, for allowing me time and resources for writing this book. Clearly it is a personal view. I am grateful to Christopher Ricks for criticizing that view. I thank Robert Merton for guidance on the development of the sociology of knowledge; Thomas Luckmann, P. Viazzo, and Jeffrey Stout for discussion of *Nuer Religion;* Thomas Kuhn for correcting the account of feedback. T. O. Beidelman's *Bibliography of the Writings of E. E. Evans-Pritchard* (1974) has been invaluable. I am grateful to Denis Hynes for help with the short bibliography and to Madeline Spitaleri for producing the finished manuscript.

BIOGRAPHICAL NOTE

1902   Born on September 21 at Crowborough, Sussex; son of the Reverend John Evans-Pritchard (Church of England) and the former Dorothea Edwards.

1916–24   Educated at Winchester College and Exeter College, Oxford, where he took an M.A. in Modern History.

1923–27   Graduate studies at the London School of Economics under B. Malinowski and C. G. Seligman.

1926–30   Fieldtrips among the Azande.

1928–31   Lecturer in Anthropology at the London School of Economics.

1930   Begins research among the Nuer.

1932   Professor of Sociology at Fuad I University (now the Egyptian University of Cairo).

1935–40   Lecturer in African Sociology at Oxford.

1939   Marries Ioma Gladys Heaton Nicholls, by whom he had three sons and two daughters.

1940–45   Military service in Ethiopia, the Sudan, and Syria.

1944   Enters Roman Catholic Church.

1945–46   Reader in Anthropology at Cambridge.

1946–70   Professor of Social Anthropology and Fellow of All Souls College at Oxford. Visiting Professor at the University of Chicago, 1950; Fellow at Center for Advanced Study in the Behavioral Sciences, Stanford, 1957–58.

1970   Retires from Chair at Oxford.

1973   Dies on September 11, in Oxford.

EDWARD EVANS-PRITCHARD

Introduction

i

"I should make it clear at this point that I am not, and never have been clever; imaginative and industrious if you like, but not clever in a bookish way of speaking. . . ."[1] So Sir Edward Evans-Pritchard in his old age described his own talents, knowing that he had achieved a resounding reputation in anthropology. The object of this book is to explain to readers unacquainted with this field what he did and why his thought is significant for the contemporary world of letters. He was a highly independent thinker who made signal advances in many branches of anthropology. His standing as a master of modern thought rests upon his solitary confronting, in the 1930s, of intellectual dilemmas that are crowding in heavily upon the social sciences forty years later.

[1] "Genesis of a Social Anthropologist," p. 18.

It is only right to say that this is not a straight summary and something different from a synthesis. I have made a personal reconstruction upon the writings, forcing them into closer confrontation with problems that were evidently present to Evans-Pritchard but which have become more public and explicit since. There was no need to go beyond Evans-Pritchard to explain the importance of his work to specialists. The challenge here is to interest others in solutions to problems they have never considered. While I was pondering how to focus on the challenge, I realized that a name for his method was missing. A name is a powerful concentrator of ideas. By naming a theory of social accountability, I can show more cogently the methodological advances that can be built only upon his work. Thus his own intention of relating moral philosophy and religion systematically with social behavior would be better fulfilled. The reader will have no difficulty, I hope, in distinguishing the master's original work from the pupil's presentation.

One of the present crises in sociology comes from the criticisms of phenomenologists. Maintaining that social understanding must start from the human experience of consciousness and reflection, they despair of truth in any so-called humane science that ignores the distinctively human element. These critics have undermined confidence in the traditional methods and even in the traditional objectives of sociology. Consequently, many scholars sensitive to the criticism have been tempted to give up striving for objectivity and to shift their own writing into a mystical mode, indulgent to their own subjectivity. Others, who would still like to try for objective comparisons, find little alternative but to work on in the old framework of inquiry, and so tend to shirk these issues. In advance of this critical juncture Evans-Pritchard felt the dilemma keenly. He would not subscribe to mechanistic social theories and resisted scientistic fashions in anthropology. His own rugged individualism forbade him to ignore individual human agency, and he found uncongenial any theorizing that reduced the mind to a mere arena in which social factors contend. It would go against his private philosophy to diminish persons in their autonomous personhood, even as objects of research, still more as objects of social engineering. But he did not abandon the wish for objective comparison. So in his own work he met the problems that now beset us all more generally. He taught that the essential point for comparison is that at which people meet misfortune. They may accuse others, they may accept responsibility. They count different kinds of misfortune as needing explanation. As they work their ideas of blame and compensation into their social institutions, they invoke existences and powers that are adapted to each particular accounting system. There are ways of getting valid evidence on these essential moral purposes as they surface from consciousness into action.

The simplest formula in which to sum up these methods and the assumptions they rest upon is tracing accountability. This book will argue that Evans-Pritchard's method of tracing notions of accountability through their institutional forms, because it starts with moral agents and their ideas about morality, shows a way out of the current difficulties in sociology. By tracing penalties and moral confrontations, a method of selecting and recording evidence emerges. The effort to classify kinds of accountability in different social systems requires a careful sifting of information. The method carries its own internal-audit system. Theoretically, payments of debt and executions of justice, when they cover the whole of social life, should tally. If they do not, there is something more to research and explain. One of the strengths of the method is that it rests on the assumption that human so-

ciety is composed not of ciphers but of active agencies
endowed with intelligence and will. Intentions create and
sustain institutions as much as institutions constrain intentions. Starting from here, the analysis opens up questions not entertained in traditional sociology.

Another feature of his modernity is Evans-Pritchard's
anticipation of the sociology of everyday knowledge. It
has been respectable to research into the history of ideas
and the sociology of knowledge since the nineteenth century. But these subjects have been venerably dressed in
capital letters, as it were, and only recently has the artificial compartmentalizing of different branches of knowledge been criticized. The phenomenological writings of
Husserl and Schutz have provoked a move to develop a
systematic sociology of the commonsense knowledge of
ordinary people in everyday contexts. Evans-Pritchard's
specialized problem in anthropology led him early to that
development because he could not deal with magic and
totemism in specialized compartments. Futhermore, he
extraordinarily anticipated the intentions of everyday-
language philosophers by his recognition of the need to
interpret speech fully in its context of functioning social
relations and especially, of course, in social accounting.

Another way in which Evans-Pritchard was in advance of his time may be no more than a curious byway
of history: but he did analyze a negative-feedback system in 1940. As the final abstraction from social reality,
system was frequently alluded to in earlier anthropological writings. Largely using neurological models as metaphors, the references were very inexact. After Norbert
Wiener worked out the principles of a feedback in his
Cybernetics (1948), it became a fashionable word, but it
was generally used in a partial sense to illustrate the
counteractive influence of different tendencies upon each
other, without defining the limits of the system nor ex-

plaining how the equivalent of an automatic control worked.[2] Evans-Pritchard worked out a systematic self-stabilizing interaction to account for otherwise inexplicable elements in the Nuer political system. There is no reason to think that his description of a feedback system in Nuer political life has further repercussions on contemporary thought. The idea may be treated as a minor invention in anthropology, though I reserve judgment against the possible day of its being more fully exploited.

I propose to justify these claims to modernity by referring to Evans-Pritchard's own work program, and to his lectures given at the Egyptian University in Cairo in the early 1930s. Here he grappled with these problems in the rough-hewn form they were then presented—as questions about the nature of primitive mentality. Now, of course, they come as questions about our own mentality. I will inevitably need to sketch in the state of the art as he had found it. Some biographical notes about his personality and fieldwork will be necessary to give an idea of the foundations of his originality.

[2] See G. Bateson, *Naven,* p. 292.

Human Mental Faculties

ii

In the 1920s, when Evans-Pritchard's training began, the central questions in anthropology related
to the conditions of human knowledge. The context for comparing tribes with each other and
with Europeans was the keen interest in the evolution of the cognitive faculties. There was no de-
limited specialism in a particular field. Anthropologists could offer ideas culled from anywhere
—zoology, physics, or primitive art. Everyone was
interested in discovering psychological or physical
or even social factors that influence perception.
How sensations coming into the brain are received, organized, and stored for retrieval by
memory, and how memory does its work were
part of a general theorizing about perceptual processes that belonged to no one narrow province.
Zoologists, psychologists, neurologists, and other
biological scientists could contribute, their results

being taken into account by philosophers. Anthropologists could introduce speculations based on the bizarre, extreme cases to which they had access. This was generally a healthy intervention, for scholars know that they are too prone to make their local experience represent the entire human race. However, one stroke in creating a division of labor leads to another. To this day, the normal cognitive processes tend to be studied in the disciplines established in the heart of our culture, while irrational or deviant forms become the special field of the scholars who report them. So totemism, magic, and taboo are assigned to anthropology, marking by their outlandish names the sidelines from which anthropologists make their contribution to understanding how the mind works.

The nineteenth-century imagination had been deeply impressed by the contrast between two of its favorite stereotypes: that of ancestral, primitive man and that of modern, scientific man. Even now the fascination of the divide remains. Among scholars who collect and sift information on the human capacity for thought, many ignore the divide but deepen it by concentrating most of their energies upon the subject nearest home. This includes the majority of those working in the sociology of knowledge, because by its history and methods sociology in general deals primarily with modern society. Then there are those thinkers whose attention is fixed precisely upon that divide. These are primarily the anthropologists. Among them some emphasize the boundary between primitive and modern ways of thought: they concentrate on elucidating words which are held to be characteristic of primitive thought, not of our own, such as taboo and totemism, which their approach treats as largely untranslatable emanations of other ways of life. Then there are anthropologists whose work seeks to lower that boundary which sets primitive thought apart from our

own. Much of Evans-Pritchard's work was devoted to re-
moving those misunderstandings about our own thought
which seem to distinguish it radically from the thought of
spear-throwing, stone-tool–using, bow-and-arrow tech-
nologists.

Nineteenth-century explorers tended to deliver extraordinary reports of the peoples they encountered.
Though the hope of fame may have driven them through
jungles and deserts hitherto unknown, many an ex-
plorer is doomed to be remembered only because of a
fish or a plant named after him, or at best by a statue in
a square. As an exception, Baron K. von den Steinen, who
explored the Amazon in the 1890s, would surely have
been gratified to know that he provided material for a
problem tough enough to exercise serious scholars for almost a hundred years. The problem arises from the
thought-provoking way he reported that the Bororo Indians of Central Brazil declared that they were red parakeets.[1] He saw at once that they could have possibly
meant that they were like red parakeets, a metaphor, or
that after death they would become red parakeets, a religious belief. He anticipated the distorting effects of
translation and tried to phrase the pertinent questions to
allow of no ambiguity. But ambiguity there was, and
when his report was repeated in 1910 by the French philosopher Lucien Lévy-Bruhl, his refinements were lost.

Lévy-Bruhl treated the Bororo as a prime example of
prelogical thinking.

> "The Bororo . . . boast that they are red araras (para-
> keets)." This does not merely signify that after their
> death they become araras, nor that araras are meta-
> morphosed Bororos, and must be treated as such. It is
> something entirely different. . . . It is not a name

[1] K. von den Steinen, *Unter der Naturvolken Zentral-Brasiliens,* p. 352 ff.

they give themselves, nor a relationship that they claim. What they desire to express by it is actual identity. That they can be both the human beings they are and the birds of scarlet plumage at the same time, von den Steinen regards as inconceivable, but to the mentality that is governed by the law of participation there is no difficulty in the matter. All communities which are totemic in form admit of collective representations of this kind, implying similar identity of the individual members of a totemic group and their totem.[2]

For Lévy-Bruhl, the Bororo capacity to tolerate self-contradiction was another case of the totally different cognitive slant, the prelogical characteristic, of primitive mentality. A number of thinkers down to the present day have made the Bororo declaration famous by quoting or trying to interpret it.[3] They are few compared with the anthropologists who have discussed totemism as a set of beliefs characteristic of peoples at a certain stage of evolution, or who have discussed similar beliefs in shared human identity with classes of animals to illustrate a general problem about cognitive differences between different cultures. Inevitably, in so much discussion, with so much evidence and relatively little sustained analysis, the contribution from the anthropologists' sidelines to the understanding of cognition has often been obfuscating. The general reader, faced by a vast and abstruse literature, may well suspect that some small detail is wrong with the explorers' reports or that something major is wrong with the theorizing. Figures of thought that would be unproblematic if located in the speech of poli-

---

[2] L. Lévy-Bruhl, *How Natives Think*, p. 62.
[3] See J. C. Crocker, "My Brother the Parrot," p. 165. See also G. Van der Leeuw, *La Structure de la Mentalité Primitive*, p. 8; R. Lowie, *History of Ethnological Theory*, p. 218; W. Percy, "The Symbolic Structure of Interpersonal Process"; L. Vygotsky, *Thought and Language*, p. 71; C. Geertz, "Religion as a Cultural System," pp. 37–38; and J. Z. Smith, "I Am a Parrot (Red)."

ticians, or (better still) in Aristotle or Shakespeare, become preposterously incompatible beliefs issuing from
the minds of primitives, creating bizarre problems which
nowadays only anthropologists take seriously.

Evans-Pritchard's entry into this discussion is that of
the plain, commensensical Englishman, trained in history, biased toward empiricism, and suspicious of grand
theoretical schemes. He brought with him two commitments: one to the unitary character of human cognition
and one to the sociological analysis that would reveal it.
The first commitment meant that he knew Lévy-Bruhl
was mistaken; that to search for a distinctively primitive
cognitive style was the wrong method for solving puzzles
such as that posed by the Bororo: if we understand ourselves better, such puzzles could be treated as problems
about our own styles of thought, so opening a shaft of
light upon the human condition. The second commitment
meant that he was determined to give a strong methodological edge to the speculations of the French sociologists
in whose writings he saw the unrealized possibilities of a
proper sociology of knowledge.

Robert Merton's review of the sociology of knowledge,
which appeared in 1945, distinguished an original German school starting from Marx and centering upon Marxist thought, a distinctively different French school whose
work he suggested was "largely autochthonous and independent of similar researches in Germany," and later
American developments.[4] Though his omission of any
British contribution is accurate, the connection between
the French and German efforts was closer than this account recognized. The German dialogue, stemming as it
did from Marxist historical materialism, was necessarily

---

[4] R. K. Merton, "The Sociology of Knowledge." The quotation
is from his "Karl Mannheim and the Sociology of Knowledge,"
p. 544.

focused on the ideological division between classes. Marx had unequivocally stated a program for the sociology of knowledge when he declared that even the definition of a problem depends on the experience of a particular historical way of living. German Marxist discussion of sociology was radical and revolutionary. If at the turn of the nineteenth century it crossed the border to France, it was understandable that it took a different focus. Moreover, France had already undergone the revolutionary bloodletting that served as a paradigm for all Europe. France had recently been invaded by Germany, and was to be so invaded twice again. The French ignored but were not ignorant of the German work. Their own approach was not so much independent but a larger response to the ideas from Germany, negating their value in the same spirit as the British psychologists denied the value of the French sociology of memory and perception. So it was that instead of being interested in class conflict, Emile Durkheim, the dominant figure in French sociology, was primarily interested in group solidarity. His synthesis of then-current theories about the social construction of categories argued that shared categories of thought are a function of and a prerequisite for society. To teach this he turned away from European history and introduced accounts of very distant, very curious small societies.

Lévy-Bruhl's theory of primitive mentality owes very little to Durkheim. (Lévy-Bruhl had actually written no less than eight books on philosophy before he turned to this topic.) He recognized that the so-called mystic participations of prelogical thought rested upon social institutions. But the occasional remarks he made about social conditions were never central to his thinking. He did not consider that his ideas needed to be developed by more research. He was satisfied to assert that primitive peoples had a different, mystical focus of attention, a different perception of relevant causal sequences, and a different logic.

Evans-Pritchard admired Lévy-Bruhl[5] and took Lévy-Bruhl's work as his own starting point in a program addressed to every anthropologist who tried to explain magic in terms of weakness in the primitive mental equipment, susceptibility to strong emotions such as awe, anxiety, or fear. The French sociologists used their notion of primitive psychology to support their position in an international and politically live argument about social solidarity, its sources and weaknesses. Evans-Pritchard would use their leading ideas to sociologize theories of the mind that hitherto had no grounding in social theory.

In many respects the Anglo-Saxon anthropologists were unsophisticated and short of learning, and it is interesting to speculate whether the political neutrality which their work enjoyed was an impediment rather than a guarantee of intellectual freedom and power. To explain the peculiarities of primitive religion they made a naïve appeal to psychology.

At Exeter College, R. R. Marett had taught a theory of the origin of religion, tracing it to a sense of awe, mystery, and wonder, to which the primitive was supposed to be particularly alive.[6] In *The Golden Bough,* Frazer traced the religious history of mankind back to a contemplative, poetic sense, an emotional view of man and nature. Malinowski explained magic as response to anxiety;[7] others explained it by fear. Elliot Smith's argument, that all cultures can be traced back to their cradle in Egypt,

---

[5] See Evans-Pritchard's note on the letter to him from L. Lévy-Bruhl ("A Letter to E. E. Evans-Pritchard").
[6] See R. Otto, *The Idea of the Holy,* and A. Lang, *The Making of Religion,* quoted in E. Sharpe, *Comparative Religion,* p. 61.
[7] See S. F. Nadel, "Malinowski on Magic and Religion," p. 195.

like other ethnological schemes of the time, had to be supported by such an elaborate theory that it fell beneath the
weight of its own implausible props.[8]

There is no need here to be more precise or more en-
cyclopedic about the exotic ideas that were invented by
Europeans to account for the newly discovered exotic beliefs of other peoples beyond the Judeo-Christian tradition. One gets the feeling that no theory would have been
too peculiar to gain some acceptance: the one needful
thing for scholarly renown was to deal with a large
enough body of evidence to be able to sweep the less
amenable information under the carpet and force the
small voice of common sense to mere piecemeal protests.
One also gets the impression that the physical scientists
who became anthropologists, perhaps for lack of a firm
foothold in the discipline of their original training, failed
to build up a solid institutional framework around their
new calling. A sense of fringy amateurishness hangs over
the pronouncements of W. R. Rivers, A. C. Haddon, Perry,
and Elliot Smith. By contrast, the French sociologists of
the same period succeeded in building up an institutional
structure that provided internal canons of criticism and
a steady development of ideas. The English were more
like freebooters who raided when they felt like it, took
only what they fancied, and furnished inaccessible hide-
outs with their scholarly loot. Nevertheless they all considered themselves to be contributing to knowledge about
human cognition.

Take for example the career of A. C. Haddon, whom
Evans-Pritchard knew well.[9] Haddon had originally been
trained as a zoologist at Cambridge. After an expedition
to Melanesia to study marine biology, he published
*The Decorative Art of New Guinea: A Study in Papuan
Ethnography* (1894). I will not stress the fact that he

[8] G. Elliot Smith, *In the Beginning.*
[9] "Genesis of a Social Anthropologist," p. 19.

plunged into art history with the most rudimentary prep-
aration. In 1895 he wrote *Evolution in Art as Illustrated
by the Life Histories of Designs*. Then in 1898–99 his
career turned over full time to ethnology when he led a
famous Cambridge expedition to Melanesia. The team he
assembled were psychologists, linguists, musicians. Its
work was from the beginning planned to contribute to
the theory of memory and perception.

Haddon's book on *Evolution in Art* is concerned, as the
title suggests, with how a design comes to life, as it were,
flourishes and gets embellished, and then simplifies, loses
its distinctive features, degenerates, and dies. We can
easily see now that the life-history approach has several
difficulties. For one, it assumes that the scholar knows
when the design is alive or dead; for another, he has already judged its degeneration by his own criteria of stability and simplification. The problem of artistic life, as
Haddon put it, is that creativity is easily overwhelmed by
inertia; we Europeans are abundantly energetic and creative, much less convention-ridden than the primitives,
known to be dull and uninventive.

For Haddon, the big divide between primitives and
moderns lay in the question: How do fruitful ideas come
to an end? The answer to the problem in art would be
the same as the answer for all civilization. Haddon in-
voked a theory of mental arrest copied on a physics model
of loss of energy, which he developed from the ideas of
Guglielmo Ferrero, an Italian. Quoting Ferrero: "By the
law of mental inertia, the state of consciousness, image,
idea, emotion . . . cannot last forever, after the exciting
cause has ceased to exist—for a state of consciousness is
a transformation of energy, and it finishes when it has
exhausted its initial quantity."[10] Haddon thought that the
life-history of a design came to a halt when the image

10 In *Evolution in Art*, pp. 300–301.

was fully standardized within a particular culture, or conventionalized. He focused attention on progressive loss of detail and loss of image, arranging his examples in a series from the richest to the simplest, showing how an alligator design or bird design could be transformed into a purely abstract scroll pattern. This process he called conventionalization.

The concept of conventionalization was immediately seized by Frederick Bartlett, the Cambridge experimental psychologist. Bartlett himself was well-read in anthropology, and some of his friends were anthropologists famous in their day. In his twenties, he later said, he had come closely under the influence of Dr. W. R. Rivers, the anthropologist, and of Dr. C. S. Myers, who was at that time the head of the Department of Experimental Psychology at Cambridge.[11] (Both Rivers and Myers had been members of Haddon's expedition to the Torres Straits in 1898.) Haddon's work on conventionalization interested Bartlett because when studying

. . . perception sequences, it seemed there came a stage when something like a stored pattern or standard representation took charge of the observer's response and principally settled what he was alleged to have perceived. Moreover, observers of much the same social group were very likely to use the same stored standard representation.

Just about this time I had become interested in the ethnographical studies of the development of decorative art forms such, for example, as those undertaken by Dr. A. C. Haddon in *The Decorative Art of New Guinea* (1894). It was from such writings that I borrowed the plan of attempting to derive and use sequences for perceiving and remembering so as to help towards an understanding of those processes of conventionalization which not only produce standards and

[11] F. C. Bartlett, *Thinking: An Experimental and Social Study,* p. 142.

patterns peculiar to the decorative art of a social group, but could also, it seemed to me, play an important part in the individual's interpretation of his own environment.

The program was now moving away from straight-forward studies of the determining activities and conditions of perceiving and remembering, towards an all-out experimental attack on conventionalizing in both its individual and its social forms.[12]

Bartlett had earlier written *Psychology and Primitive Culture* (1923) in which he quoted many American and British anthropologists. His book started out with the assumption, established in philosophy and psychology, that the process of cognition is a selective screening and organizing of sensory inputs. But he was unusual in insisting that, the individual subject being always a social individual, the selective screening must be influenced by social experiences. He worked this out with many ethnographic examples. His analysis of the folk tale is particularly convincing: the search for the origins of a folk tale is futile; likewise the discovery of those grand archetypal themes dear to many psychologists, or the attempt to use folk tales to establish the history of past institutions. He said firmly:

It is not the institution that is derived from the story, but the story from the institution. . . . That the folk story is a social product implies, among other things, that in its matter the popular tale must make a common-sense appeal and in its form it must be shaped as to call forth a widely readily shared response. *For both of these characters spring from the fact that the folk story is largely a mode of social intercourse.*[13] [My italics.]

Bartlett had important insights on taboo, which he insisted was not to be blamed by fear. Many writers of the

[12] Ibid., p. 143.
[13] *Psychology and Primitive Culture*, p. 63.

time named fear as the primary emotion explaining ta-
boos. "But when we turn to popular stories . . . descriptions of fear seem to occupy no very important position."[14]
Bartlett himself explained taboo by a sociological require-
ment to control conflict by separating spheres of action
and even creating separate cognitive spheres. For "the
general determination of boundaries" and for the social
control of curiosity, Bartlett's words were remarkably explicit: "The history of any primitive group, in fact, reveals certain spheres of activity within which curiosity is
not readily to be allowed full sway. The limitation does
not necessarily produce disorder. Curiosity is assigned to
its own realm."[15]

This was a book to put into the hands of anthropologists; it was full of good sense and promise for a sociological approach to perception. In it, Bartlett had been
fully committed to solving the problem of how social
factors influence cognition. He knew and accepted that
the problem of conventionalization could be solved only
by knowing the institutions in which conventional responses were embedded. He had said so over and over
again. However, when he went on later to write his justly
famous book *Remembering* (1932), he had made very
little progress toward a sociological theory of cognition.

Working on the psychology of memory, he planned to
expand and test the idea—held by the neurologist Henry
Head—that each individual attends selectively to sensations whose stored results create a cumulatively developed schema. Head supposed the schema or armature of
attention to be individual, but, as we have seen, Bartlett
expected it to be institutionally anchored. He said of the
attempted draft of a book about conventionalizing:
"There came a time when I began to write this book, and
I labored heavily through two or three chapters, but it

[14] Ibid., p. 110.
[15] Ibid., pp. 117–18.

did not go well. I tore up what I had written and for some time there followed a most unpleasant period when it seemed that I had taken a lot of steps to get nowhere at all."

The young genius Norbert Wiener, who "was at that time in Cambridge studying mathematical logic," brought the barren period to an end by helpfully suggesting that the "Russian Scandal" game be turned into an experimental method. An experimental subject was isolated and shown a picture; the picture then being taken away, the subject was asked to reproduce it. His drawing was then presented to the next subject who saw it equally briefly, lost it, and was asked to reproduce what he recalled, and so on, until as many subjects as were required had worked on successive transformations of the original design. By this means he could show some of the perceptual processes that lead to a steady reproduction or to conventionalization.[16]

By two ideas, serial reproduction and subjective organization of experience, Bartlett had found a way of exploring memory and, through memory, recognition and other faculties of the mind. The work he then embarked on was immense. Each experiment that he counted successful led him to consider new ones. An inventor of methodologies and a supreme instrument-maker, he succeeded in showing how the perceiving subject organizes, constructs, maintains, and defends the stability of its cognitive scheme. There was so much work to do in developing this approach that he relegated the program of discovering the social foundation of stable perception. So he himself fulfilled his life-work's lesson. He had taught originally that social institutions accounted for memory and forgetting. The author of the best book on remembering forgot his own first convictions. He became

[16] F. C. Bartlett, *Thinking*, p. 144

absorbed into the institutional framework of Cambridge University psychology and restricted by the conditions of the experimental laboratory.

Bartlett's work is relevant here because it establishes the claim that anthropology was expected to contribute to psychology in the 1920s and that close exchanges were made between those disciplines. It also illustrates the difficulty of creating a sociological theory of perception, and helps to explain why such a theory is still missing to this day.

A reason for picking out Haddon and Bartlett to illustrate this earlier period, rather than Rivers, Radcliffe-Brown, or Malinowski, is the evidence that Evans-Pritchard adopted Bartlett's research interests and even used the same vocabulary about selective principles of attention for indicating what he held to be the central problems. He is also the only anthropologist in England whose work provides this continuous relationship with a major concern in perception psychology.

At that period the most popular models for the processes of human reasoning were borrowed from the physical sciences, and the best were neurological. In addition to Henry Head, Charles Sherrington was enormously influential for anthropology. He worked out the neural connections in the spinal column and brain stem that sustain the normal maintenance of muscle tone and of posture and reflex movements in the limbs. Then, moving on from the spinal column and brain stem to the forebrain of the cat and ape, he mapped the motor keyboard of the cerebral cortex. His main theme was to insist on the total integration of the nervous system.[17]

So many of Sherrington's concepts were borrowed, extended, and transformed by thinkers in other fields that it is impossible to separate threads in what became a

[17] *The Integrative Action of the Nervous System,* 1906.

common canopy of ideas. Take his demonstration of reciprocal innervation, the principle by which antagonistic
muscles must relax to allow the contraction of the muscles that cause a limb to move. In sociology, Bartlett tried
to focus on "group difference" tendencies that clustered
about various forms of institutions, and insisted that it is
not enough to know what these tendencies are: one must
also study the relationship they bear to one another;
particularly, he was interested in the "conflict of tendencies and their mutual reinforcement,"[18] and in processes
of inhibiting antagonism. This sounds so like a vague
version of Freud's model of the mind, as well as Sherrington's neurological model, that it is clear that the
basic idea of reciprocal interplay between forces was
freely available to contemporary thought.

An important disseminator of Sherrington's ideas in
the 1920s was Eugenio Rignano (1870–1930). An Italian
professor of philosophy who wrote on many topics and
was quickly translated into French and English, Rignano
worked out what he called a mnemonic explanation of
attention. He had a systemic theory of mental functions:
the whole organism was always involved, he argued, and
for a human being the concept of the whole organism
would have to include its social ambience. He took over
Sherrington's distinction between nondistance perceptors
(which "permit immediate or almost immediate satisfac-
tion of the affective tendencies with which they start")
and distance perceptors (which can hold the state of
attention in suspense). Among Rignano's examples: the
sea anemone does not pay attention or react to the presence of food except when its metabolism has reached a
state requiring more nutrient. In man, the experience of
hunger, a particular localized sensation in the wall of the

18 See *Psychology and Primitive Culture*, ch. 4.

stomach, is enough to cause the same acts that would
be induced by real hunger. Long before starvation is
threatened, the immediate perception of hunger has re-
minded the human organism that it needs nourishment;
long before death from thirst, a local sensation in the
mouth and throat is a warning request for attention; the
species will die out if not reproduced, but the sexual urge
is called into action without waiting for the species' sur-
vival to be at risk. Rignano said that in these forms we
find the substitution of the part for the whole: thirst and
sexual hunger are examples of the mnemonic process by
which the needs of the whole organism are continually
met by short-lived local transfers of attention—early-
warning reminders, as it were.

The array of slow and quick nerve pathways to the
brain, the concept of reciprocal innervation, the power
to suspend attention—these three ideas appear later in
Evans-Pritchard's work. At least his debt here can be
tracked, for several times he acknowledged Rignano's
book *The Psychology of Reasoning.* He even placed Rignano alongside William James in his programmatic statement about the need to understand the selective principles controlling attention. On this issue, the difference
between Evans-Pritchard and anyone else in England
(apart from Bartlett) was his confidence that the selective principles were to be found in social institutions, and
that fieldwork was the way to find them. Seen in this
light, his life-work can be presented as a tribute to the
French sociologists, Durkheim, Mauss,[19] Lévy-Bruhl, and
Halbwachs,[20] potential collaborators who worked on the
same problems of perception but were rejected by psychologists on the English side of the Channel.[21] The

[19] M. Mauss, "Les Techniques du Corps."
[20] M. Halbwachs, "La Mémoire Collective chez les Musiciens."
[21] Bartlett, *Remembering.*

failure of British psychologists to develop a sociological dimension to their experimental thinking and the failure of the French to benefit from the British methodological advances are themselves problems for the sociology of knowledge that are not explained by their not knowing of each other's work. They read, but they misunderstood.

The Continuity of Evans-Pritchard's Program

This statement, made in 1934, may be taken as a summary of the theoretical interests and the field in which Evans-Pritchard intended to work:

> As James, Rignano, and others have shown, any sound or sight may reach the brain of a person without entering into his consciousness. We may say that he "hears" or "sees" it but does not "notice" it. In a stream of sense impressions only a few become conscious impressions and these are selected on account of their greater affectivity. A man's interests are the selective agents and these are to a great extent socially determined for it is generally the value attached to an object by all members of a social group that directs the attention of an individual towards it.
>
> It is, therefore, a mistake to say that savages perceive mystically or that their perception is mystical. On the other hand we may say that savages pay attention to phenomena on ac-

count of the mystical properties with which their society has endowed them, and that often their interest in phenomena is mainly, even exclusively, due to these mystic properties.[1]

The statement points to society as the whole field of human interests and thus as the source of the selective principle that controls attention.

In planning this book, trying to work out his intellectual origins, I checked Evans-Pritchard's footnotes and bibliographic references. In his later writing, marked punctiliousness in gratefully acknowledging every missionary's or district officer's evidence on every conceivable fieldwork topic seemed to be paralleled by virtual silence as to his intellectual debts. The relation of his ethnographic researches to contemporary speculations or theory was never spelled out in his big fieldwork monographs. As a matter of principle these were written with practically no polemics, no controversies, no disputatious threshing out of definitions. Evans-Pritchard did not think it right to use the ethnographic reporting as a forum for personal triumphs against rival theories. The task of ethnographic presentation was too solemn and too difficult. The anthropologist had to use his scholarly and sociological sense to present a coherent story, omitting nothing, twisting nothing, and adding nothing that could not be justified. The theoretical burden would be found in the internal consistency of a large body of ethnographic analysis, in which other ethnographers would discern theoretical innovation. In his big books on the Nuer, the Azande, and the Bedouin there is little guidance to the layman as to what they were meant to contribute to twentieth-century controversy. Later general statements in pamphlets and papers written after his fieldwork days were over, were written for students and

[1] "Lévy-Bruhl's Theory of Primitive Mentality," p. 24.

the general public; their style is bland, as if everything were terribly obvious. But reflection on his whole opus made me realize that the life-plan of intellectual effort had already been mapped out very clearly in the three essays published in the *Bulletin of the Faculty of Arts* of the Egyptian University: "The Intellectualist (English) Interpretation of Magic," (1933); "Lévy-Bruhl's Theory of Primitive Mentality" (1934), and "Science and Sentiment: An Exposition and Criticism of the Writings of Pareto" (1936). These essays are mature, considered statements of the program on which Evans-Pritchard was already well-embarked. The students of the Faculty of Arts of Fuad I University had been privileged to hear their teacher's long-term agenda of publications explained and justified. Here we get plenty of controversy, denunciations, sarcasm, hard-hitting argumentation. On the evidence of these essays, Evans-Pritchard fully intended his work as a major contribution to a sociological theory of knowledge.

The first essay was on the subject of magic. It would be easier and more in the mood of this exercise to use the word foreign where "primitive" or "savage" ways of thought are referred to. But it would be worse than a mere anachronism to do so. The charge of weak logic or impaired reasoning faculties gained all its interest precisely because it was not laid to the door of all foreigners but applied to people called primitive and therefore in some sense like our forebears. The notion that their minds were still in thrall to magic romanticized the subject, while it justified its seriousness by suggesting evolutionary trends to which all human society was supposedly subject. It will be necessary to use the terms "primitive thought" and "primitive magic," though Evans-Pritchard's own work should by now have dismantled the difference.

Magic was the one word that focused the discussion in his day. Primitives believed in magic, and we did not. Magic contrasted with the style of thought in a modern Western-type society, technologically superior, with its knowledge of the external world soundly based on scientific principles. But it was important, said Evans-Pritchard, to clarify the point that scientific thought is a very specialized experience that only takes place in very specialized conditions. Those who engage in it do not engage in it all the time: when they are out of the laboratory they think like everyone else does every day. The contrast between primitives and ourselves is much exaggerated by pretending that we think scientifically all the time. To prevent that error the proper method is to compare like with like, our everyday thought with their everyday thought. Immediately the investigation is shifted to a lower level. Everyday language and everyday thought set into their situational context have to be the subject of inquiry. Not only do we not conduct our lives as if we were conducting scientific experiments, but we do not think about the subject matter of religion as if we were theologians. The anthropological discussion had become hopelessly obfuscated by false and arbitrary abstractions. Particularly, the cogitations of the primitive upon his luck, his hopes, his death, and judgment (no more jumbled, nor less, than our own upon the same subjects) had been erected into a complex structure of thought. Worthy of the name philosophy only by virtue of its complexities, a total fabrication of the investigator, primitive thought was never a philosophy subscribed to by anyone at any time, but the result of weary replies to relentless interrogators who knew from their own religious background what questions to ask and what answers to count or discount. So a crazy patchwork theorizing, put together by the mind of the inquirer, was doing duty for the primitive in contrast with an equally unrealistic representation of modern thought.

For example, Evans-Pritchard said:

> [Lévy-Bruhl] was not really comparing what savages think with what Europeans think but the systematized ideology of savage cultures with the content of individual minds in Europe. His authorities had collected all the information they could get about the mystical beliefs held by a community of savages about some phenomenon and pieced them together into a coordinated ideological structure. These beliefs, like the myths which Europeans also record, may have been collected over a long period of time and from dozens of informants. The resulting pattern of belief may be a fiction since it may never be actually present in a man's consciousness at any time and may not even be known to him in its entirety. This fact would have emerged if records of everything a savage does and says throughout a single day were recorded, for then we would be able to compare our own thoughts more adequately with the real thoughts of savages instead of with an abstraction pieced together from persistent enquiries conducted in an atmosphere quite unlike that of the savage's ordinary milieu and in which it is the European who evokes the beliefs by his questions rather than the objects with which they are associated. . . . Moreover, primitive thought as pieced together in this manner by European observers is full of contradictions which do not arise in real life because the bits of belief are evoked in different situations.[2]

He makes the same complaint against Pareto:

> Pareto . . . intends to study the part played by logical, and the part played by non-logical, thought and behaviour side by side, and in interaction, in the same culture. His intention was excellent. In fact, however, he does not adhere to this plan. He writes at great length about fallacious beliefs and irrational behaviour

[2] Ibid., pp. 28–29.

but he tells us very little about common-sense beliefs and empirical behaviour. . . . If Pareto for civilized peoples, and Lévy-Bruhl for savages, had given us a detailed account of their real life during an ordinary day we would be able to judge whether their non-logical behaviour is as qualitatively and quantitatively important as the writers' selective methods would lead us to suppose. Actually, I would contend, non-logical conduct plays a relatively minor part in the behaviour of either primitive or civilized men and is relatively of minor importance.[3]

Note Evans-Pritchard's demand for an account of real life in an ordinary day and the rejection of misleading distinctions between primitives and moderns.

Pareto's work is an amusing commentary on Lévy-Bruhl's books. Lévy-Bruhl has written several volumes to prove that savages are pre-logical in contrast to Europeans who are logical. Pareto has written several volumes to prove that Europeans are non-logical. It would therefore seem that no one is mainly controlled by reason anywhere or at any epoch.[4]

Here in embryo is Evans-Pritchard's critique of the concepts of reason and rationality as the philosophers use the terms. "Indeed one of the reasons why I have chosen to analyse Pareto's treatise is to bring out the fact that a study of unscientific thought and ritual behaviour cannot be restricted to primitive societies but must be extended to civilized societies also."[5] Evans-Pritchard's method requires common sense to be compared with common sense, ritual with ritual, theology with theology so that the appropriate level may be kept. In its full development the method requires the context of belief and behavior to be specified. Demanding the social context for interpreting

[3] "Science and Sentiment," p. 184.
[4] Loc. cit.
[5] Ibid., p. 185.

verbal utterances was Malinowski's great teaching.[6] But Evans-Pritchard was to go much further in defining social contexts. At this early stage, he explicitly praised Lévy-Bruhl for perceiving that the publicly known clusters of ideas that he called collective representations "are functions of institutions, so that we may suppose as social structures vary, the collective representations will show concomitant variations."[7] But Lévy-Bruhl did not follow up the implications of this remarkable quotation. In fact, Evans-Pritchard seems to have set him up as a straw man, for Lévy-Bruhl had surely not realized the significance of the sociological remarks he occasionally threw in or he could not have written so much about prelogical mentality. Evans-Pritchard makes these failings quite clear.

> . . . Whom is one to accuse of "prelogical mentality," the South African missionaries or the Negroes of whom they record that "they only believe what they see" and that "in the midst of the laughter and applause of the populace, the heathen enquirer is heard saying 'Can the God of the white men be seen with our eyes?' " . . . Both missionaries and Negroes alike were dominated by the collective representations of their cultures. Both were alike critical when their thought was not determined by social doctrines.[8]

In these three early lectures, Evans-Pritchard dismissed the terms "illogical," "nonlogical" and "prelogical" from the discussion of primitive mentality. Scientific thought was not to be recognized merely by living with its results in a technologically advanced society. At this stage he followed Pareto's division of thought into two categories, the logico-experimental and the nonlogico-experimental: the former is scientific and the latter is

---

[6] See B. Malinowski, *Coral Gardens and Their Magic,* Vol. II.
[7] "Lévy-Bruhl's Theory of Primitive Mentality," p. 3.
[8] Ibid., pp. 8–10.

not. But it was still necessary to insist that thought that is coherently built up from valid inferences is not necessarily defective in logic; with irreproachable logic it can be very defective in its description of reality from the point of view of any foreign culture. If the premises are different, equally correct reasoning will lead to a different picture of the world.

At this stage of the argument, Evans-Pritchard felt he needed a definition of scientific notions; he derived it from his own cultural tradition.[9] Standing square to the ontology of his own culture, he felt able to use the word mystical for beliefs in entities and powers that did not enter into the logico-experimental account of objective reality. He stayed with that word to the last, finding it useful, even though he had long since discarded the word supernatural.[10] But when he uses mystical there is no hint of derogatory judgment. Those experiences which the scientific culture cannot include within objective reality are labeled mystical, but not judged either real or unreal. He made a great point of taking their reality as seriously as do the people who create and live with mystic powers and entities.

We would surely not wish our idea about the nature of reality to be frozen at any one particular moment in the development of science. Might it not have been wiser for Evans-Pritchard to have kept silent altogether about objective reality? Some philosophical commentators have used his work to support their denial that systematic comparisons between cultures is possible. This is just as contrary to his thought as it is mistaken to use his work for imagining cultures based on alternative logic or on nonlogical thinking. Evans-Pritchard believed in making comparison possible and expected it to be possible by

[9] "Science and Sentiment," p. 188.
[10] "The Intellectualist (English) Interpretation of Magic," p. 311.

studying different responses to misfortune. His method of research implicitly anchored each local version of reality to the local system of accountability.

It is good to pause here to observe how Evans-Pritchard's own independent reasoning brought him to two principles enunciated in Wittgenstein's *Philosophical Investigations* and much cited as clues to the latter's work. Both thinkers were forced to struggle out of the toils of existing speculative formulations, and both saw that the meanings of thoughts and words had to be located in social activity.

Evans-Pritchard was in the middle of fieldwork when he delivered his lectures in Egypt, but he had not yet written the first of his books. In the lectures he straightened out the then-current entanglements. The program he wrote for himself would abhor speculative abstractions; there would be evidence for everything he reported. The facts would not be selected by subjective bias; they would not be selected from hundreds of societies. The evidence would not be hearsay; it would not be elicited by interrogation; it would not be purely verbal. Assuming that words and ideas are inextricable from the rest of social action, an interpretation would be upheld by complete description of the rules governing the action in which the speech occurs.

Looking back at his work as a whole and trying to trace the main influences on him, it seems extraordinary that he did not know what Wittgenstein was saying, or how closely they paralleled each other. But apparently the convergence results not from contact but from similar historical pressures. Once the trail is laid, anyone who reads the *Philosophical Investigations* will see even richer convergences, and further implications from Evans-Pritchard's scrupulous working out of a method and its philosophy.

First, take Wittgenstein's insistence that the speaking of a language is part of activity and that it only makes sense when the rest of the activity is known: ". . . the term 'language-game' is meant to bring into prominence that the speaking of a language is part of an activity, or of a form of life." "Think of the tools in a box. . . ." Searching for a meaning is "like looking into a cabin of a locomotive." It is "easy to think of a language consisting only of orders and reports in battle."[11] Then there is the distinction to be made between on the one hand the core of fundamental assumptions (the total system of hypotheses) and on the other hand the inductive reasoning that it makes possible. Deep assumptions about the universe that arise from how people live together are unchallengeable and largely un-inspectable. Somewhere reasoning has to come to an end; it stops at these assumptions. Why are the heathen enquirers so certain that they are right and the missionary's story is wrong? Because they have to live and act: action proceeds upon decisions and decisions upon assumptions, but the assumptions anticipate possibilities of action. "Whether the earlier experience is the cause of the certainty depends on the system of hypotheses, of natural laws, in which we are considering the phenomenon of certainty. Is our confidence justified?—What people accept as justification—is shown by how they think and live." "We expect this, and are surprised *at that*. But the chain of reasoning has an end."[12] That it has to have an end is reasonable enough; but how it comes to an end and what that end is like, how it can be recognized, is not foreseen in the *Philosophical Investigations* or in the many commentaries upon it. Evans-Pritchard's method of tracing meanings through the process of fixing human accountability un-

[11] *Philosophical Investigations*, pars. 23, 11, 12, 19.
[12] Ibid., pars. 325, 326.

covers the fundamental system of hypotheses, both where the chain of reasoning stops and where its links are forged.

Many anthropologists, even recently, have adopted the theory of knowledge that Wittgenstein attributed to Saint Augustine, one in which words are assumed to correlate with, or stand for, particular meanings. The result is a triad containing reality, a set of concepts about reality, and a system of signs that signify the concepts: meaning is turned into a limited item, or at least a limited set of possible transformations, and much philosophical inquiry has focused upon the relation between the case as it is and the case that is given in the concepts. Wittgenstein tried to shift the focus of inquiry from an abstracted set of concepts, chosen and groomed to be worked upon by philosophers, towards the idea of meanings generated in active exchanges within the framework of human intentions. The value of knowledge is to be found not in its firm anchorage in some postulated fixed reality, but in its service within the rules devised for achieving some human ends. The entanglements of philosophy come from false abstractions, taking thoughts out of context and giving thought to thoughts about thoughts: "Like an engine idling, not when it is doing work."[13] This exactly parallels Evans-Pritchard on the overformalization and false abstractions of Frazer and Lévy-Bruhl. Of clarifications in philosophy, Wittgenstein said: "What we are de-destroying is nothing but houses of cards, and we are clearing up the ground of language on which they stand. The results of philosophy are the uncovering of one or another piece of plain nonsense and bumps that the understanding has got by running its head up against the limits of language."[14]

[13] Ibid., par. 132.
[14] Ibid., par. 125.

If we follow closely Evans-Pritchard's methods along this same path, we will find some of Wittgenstein's enigmas clarified. Anthropology can add something to the idea of the limits of knowledge, or the "limits of the world," a reiterated phrase in Wittgenstein. Evans-Pritchard had a method to contribute to the idea of perspicuous representation (or the transparent proof and overview which carries conviction); he had something to say about the grounds or conditions that make knowledge possible; and he said something positive about the possibilities of comparison between societies that had been doubted by Wittgenstein's followers. At these points Evans-Pritchard's work entered a conversation for which it was ready but in whose cogs it has not even yet been fully engaged. He started by seeking the selective principles governing attention, and started (thanks to the French colleagues) by expecting the principles to lie in social interaction. He had to cut through the methodological entanglements we have described; this greatly increased his sensitivity to the question of what can be taken as evidence. In his dealing with that question he opened the other doors one by one.

Fieldwork Methods

iv

It would be easy for an English anthropologist, coming after Malinowski and taking the perspectives of the French sociologists of *L'Année Sociologique* seriously, to see that the next step would have to be the systematic gathering of information by rigorously controlled methods. Evans-Pritchard's Egyptian essays show clearly how defective were the sources currently being used in all anthropological controversies.

In the history of anthropology, new stages in the development of fieldwork provide just as distinctive markers of new periods as the development of telescopes in astronomy. Before the turn of the century the main sources of information for anthropology were the detailed monographs of missionaries who had spent their lives among the people whose customs they wrote about. The anthropologists who pondered upon these materials came from literary, classical, and legal studies. They corresponded with the travelers, merchants, administrators, and missionaries, and interpreted their reports according to the current theories. No one thought of doing systematic fieldwork. Indeed a naïve belief persisted that the facts collected and combined in this way into theories were somehow pure facts, unbiased by theory-making. The two processes, collecting facts and theorizing, were held to be as different as spinning and weaving, with a more resounding glory to be earned by the weaver of theories.[1] Heaven forbid! Sir James Frazer had replied to William James's inquiry about natives he might have known himself.[2]

Eventually library analysis gave way to the next stage, when physical scientists replaced the literary philosophers in anthropology. Boas, a physicist and geographer led expeditions to Baffin Island and British Columbia A. C. Haddon, as we have seen, originally a marine biologist, led an expedition to Melanesia in 1898. With him went experts in psychology, medicine, linguistics, and music. C. G. Seligman was one of those who accompanied Haddon to Melanesia; he later organized surveys of African cultures on which he employed Evans-Pritchard as research assistant.

The next development, after the grand surveys and expeditions, led to the full professionalization of anthropology as a career. This was inaugurated by Malinowski, who is recognized as the father of modern anthropology because of his high standards for fieldwork.[3] Evans-Pritchard, however, insisted that Malinowski share the credit with A. R. Radcliffe-Brown, saying that the latter,

[1] See H. Balfour, *Spinners and Weavers in Anthropological Research*.
[2] E. Evans-Pritchard, *Social Anthropology*, p. 72.
[3] See R. Firth, ed., *Man and Culture: An Evaluation of the Work of Bronislaw Malinowski*.

being much the abler thinker, had been the first to do intensive fieldwork within a sociological framework of ideas and had described the social life of the Andaman Islanders with some kind of theoretical position to develop. Malinowski had indubitably spent much longer in one study of a single people, the Trobriand Islanders of Melanesia. He spent the years of World War I in their midst. He was the first anthropologist to conduct his research through the native language and the first to live in the center of the life he was recording: "In these favorable circumstances Malinowski came to know the Trobriand Islanders well, and he was describing their social life in a number of bulky and some shorter monographs up to the time of his death."[4] This halfhearted praise implied it was a piece of luck to get the credit for developing a new method just because of an enforced stay of four years among delightful palm trees and lagoons, with barely two theoretical notions to rub together, no formulated problems, no sharp cutting edge for any investigation, and no controlled comparisons.

Between Radcliffe-Brown's greater theoretical strength and his weaknesses in fieldwork, and Malinowski's theoretical softness and field strength, Evans-Pritchard, writing this comparison, could have felt his own record of African fieldwork made a fair bid to surpass them both at their best. His study of the Azande was based on twenty months of fieldwork. His research among the Nuer totaled only one year. But each expedition was organized so systematically that one aspect of life analyzed in detail contributed to understanding another and another until a consistent picture emerged in the round. He made six field expeditions and wrote briefly upon other peoples of the Sudan. In World War II, as political officer to the British Administration of Cyrenaica, in Libya, he

[4] *Social Anthropology*, p. 74.

collected the historical and ethnographic information for a book on the Sanusiya, an Islamic religious order. Others have spent more time in fieldwork, spread their energies over more areas, or concentrated more single-mindedly upon one small place; but none, I think, has so systematically organized the ethnography of a cultural region and brought to three intensive studies such a sustained inquiry.

Working for C. G. Seligman, Evans-Pritchard first conducted ethnological surveys in the Sudan. This meant tracing the territorial spread of a people, mapping the boundaries of their language and culture, and the boundaries of their political domain. Such a survey was normally carried out very quickly, with visits lasting from one day to a few weeks at the outside, using questioning, working through interpreters and selected informants. After he had helped to collect information for Seligman's *Survey of the Pagan Tribes of the Nilotic Sudan*, Evans-Pritchard started real fieldwork. According to his own teaching the anthropologist

> must live as far as possible in their villages and camps, where he is, again as far as possible, physically and morally part of the community. . . . This is not merely a matter of physical proximity. There is also a psychological side to it. By living among the natives as far as he can like one of themselves the anthropologist puts himself on a level with them. Unlike the administrator and missionary he has no authority and status to maintain, and unlike them he has a neutral position. He is not there to change their way of life but as a humble learner of it; and he has no retainers and intermediaries who obtrude between him and the people, no police, interpreters, or catechists to screen him off from them.[5]

Colonel Larken, the district commissioner, has described how Evans-Pritchard worked:

[5] Ibid., pp. 78–79.

He immediately plunged straight into Zande life, though speaking no Zande, and having, as his servants, boys that spoke no other language. It was his idea that this drastic method would force him to pick up the language more quickly than any other, and that while he was doing so he would be able to absorb the local atmosphere. He had his house built in one of Chief Gangura's villages, and lived a most uncomfortable life, doing it deliberately to get close to the people he wished to observe. He was remarkably quick in learning enough Zande to start his interrogations, which he pursued with intense and most conscientious care. . . . His sympathetic approach and friendliness endeared him to all, and his manner was an ideal one for persuading them to tell him anything he wished to know.

With his knowledge for a guide, one can now form a just appreciation of Zande actions and reactions which might otherwise appear incomprehensible or even blameworthy. No doubt many people will, thanks to him, escape unjust punishments, and receive a favourable response to their often obscure requests.[6]

From Evans-Pritchard's writing it is easy to guess now what these obscure requests were about: the everyday thought of the Azande was dominated by a theory of misfortune caused by witchcraft, and their other anxieties were all ultimately translatable into a concern to work the oracles that would warn them of witchcraft and to obtain the magic to fend it off or punish it.

Carrying out his precepts to the letter, Evans-Pritchard even conducted his own life by following the advice of oracles. He said that he took care "to enact the same procedure as Azande and to take oracular verdicts as they take them. I always kept a supply of poison for the use of my household and we regulated our affairs in accordance with the oracle's decision. I may say that I

[6] Quoted as dedication in A. Singer and B. V. Street, eds., *Zande Themes; Essays Presented to Sir Edward Evans-Pritchard.*

found it as satisfactory a way of running my home and affairs as any other I know of."[7]

He had chosen the Azande for his first major fieldwork because he was attracted by their friendly sophistication. His next fieldwork was no choice of his. An urgent request from the government of the Sudan called him to report on an unruly Nilotic tribe whose insurrection would be put down by force unless someone could interpret their intentions. He says that he agreed only after hesitation and misgivings: "I was anxious to complete my study of the Azande before embarking on a new task. I also knew that a study of the Nuer would be extremely difficult. Their country and character are alike intractable and what little I had previously seen of them convinced me that I would fail to establish friendly relations with them."[8]

However, Evans-Pritchard felt he had a responsibility as an anthropologist, because there was the risk that unless some trusted means of communication could be established the Nuer would fight until they were destroyed. His assessment of the difficulties was right. But it now seems that nothing had happened to him before, that he had hardly started to discover his own humanity and the height of his powers until he lived among the Nuer. This is the dedication to his first book on them:

Ah, the land of the rustling of wings, which is beyond the rivers of Ethiopia: that sendeth ambassadors by the sea, even in vessels of papyrus upon the waters (saying) Go ye swift messengers, to a nation tall and smooth, to a people terrible from their beginning onward; a nation that meteth out and treadeth down, whose land the rivers divide.

(Isaiah xviii: 1–2)

[7] *Witchcraft, Oracles, and Magic among the Azande*, p. 220.
[8] *The Nuer*, pp. 8–9.

When he had completed his last volume on the Nuer, he seems to lay down the pen with a sigh of fulfillment:

> It is sad that I must now say a final farewell to a people who have for so many years occupied my thoughts. I was . . . an alien sojourner, among them for only a year, but it was a year's relation of great intensity, and the quality of a relationship counts far more than its duration. This final volume of my trilogy is dedicated to them in memory of an experience which has greatly influenced my life.[9]

Even the short account I will give of the theoretical insights he gained through working with them will be suggestive of what they meant to him. The Nuer forced him to carry out his own precepts: to be respectful of the people he was studying; to be humble before them, an equal and no more; to depend on them. The twelve months' total of fieldwork was scraped together, seven weeks here, three months there, another month somewhere else, and then back again: it was continually hindered or interrupted by illness, by political difficulties ("A government force surrounded our camp one morning at sunrise, searched for two prophets who had been leaders in a recent revolt"), by drought, by diplomatic delays.

In their way of initiating him to their life Nuer were like Zen masters, mocking and cruel, childish and clever at once. Eventually he and they crossed the dividing distance between them:

> As I became more friendly with the Nuer and more at home in their language they visited me from early morning till late at night, and hardly a moment of the day passed without men, women, or boys in my tent. . . . These endless visits entailed constant badinage and interruption and, although they offered opportunity for improving my knowledge of the Nuer lan-

[9] *Nuer Religion*, p. ix.

guage, imposed a severe strain. Nevertheless, if one chooses to reside in a Nuer camp one must submit to Nuer custom, and they are persistent and tireless visitors. The chief privation was the publicity to which all my actions were exposed, and it was long before I became hardened, though never entirely insensitive, to performing the most intimate operations before an audience or in full view of the camp. . . . Azande would not allow me to live as one of themselves; Nuer would not allow me to live otherwise. Among Azande I was compelled to live outside the community; among Nuer I was compelled to be a member of it. Azande treated me as a superior; Nuer as an equal.[10]

Among the Azande he interrogated, among the Nuer he could only gather information in particles, not "in chunks supplied by selected and trained informants." No sneaking British love for amateurism has slipped in here. The new professionalism in fieldwork was not to rely on trained informants—it was to use participant observation first and formulate questions afterward in the light of field experiences. But this is not to say that the new fieldwork was unsystematic. On the contrary, the village census, the genealogy, the biography became established methods of checking and validating what might otherwise seem to be subjective impressions.[11]

The trail of Evans-Pritchard's fieldwork itself is a guide to his own development. From the crafty, charming Azande, who considered every neighbor to be a potential witch and calmly took magic measures to combat witchcraft dangers, he learned to expand his West European view of rationality to include worlds built upon other assumptions than we subscribe to. Going from the Azande to the Nuer, he had to reformulate the careful boundaries he had earlier drawn between mystic and rational, every-

[10] *The Nuer*, pp. 14–15.
[11] See "Some Aspects of Marriage and Family among the Nuer."

day reason and scientific thinking. Naked and simple, the Nuer opened vistas of other constructed universes, richer, nobler, and better substantiated than any in Europe's romantic visions of the savage. After the Nuer he was ready to encounter Islam. In 1944 he entered the Roman Catholic Church. Some have regarded this step as a change of direction, but he insisted that it was no sudden break with his past but the latest step in the steady development of one who had always been a Catholic at heart.[12]

A historian might say that some anthropologist was bound to feel the pressure to combine the traditions of French speculative theorizing and English fieldworking empiricism. This would be a deterministic approach to the history of ideas. Evans-Pritchard's own approach to sociology was antideterministic; he focused on men's purposes and their choices in dealing with one another. Indeed his career was very much the product of personal choices, not of impersonal convergent forces. This is the place to enter a comment on the personality of the anthropologist. He chose to combine the work of a scholar conversant with many languages with the life of a man of action, traveled in many lands.[13] He praised desert landscapes, loved Persian poetry, and could recite reams of it by heart in English translation. He himself translated Arabic hymns and elegies into a style of English verse that confirmed the remark that his taste in poetry was Victorian and romantic.[14] His gift for friendship was enriched by extraordinary intuition and sensitivity.

A good insight into his attitudes comes from reading his *Sanusi of Cyrenaica* (1949). The interruption of research imposed by wartime military service in Syria and

[12] See "Fragment of an Autobiography," p. 37.
[13] See "Genesis of a Social Anthropologist," p. 18.
[14] See G. Lienhardt, "E. P.: A Personal View," p. 304.

Libya had renewed the contact with Bedouin Arabs begun with his teaching in Egypt ten years before. He evidently rejoiced in the chance to be immersed in Arabic civilization. Before writing the next outstanding book on the Nuer he paid a debt to Islam. Better than anything else he wrote, his history of the Sanusi Order in Cyrenaica explains his recurrent shafts of criticism against reductionist theorizing and against sociological determinism. By a tour de force his combination of anthropology and history paid tribute to great personalities, so making explicit the voluntarist principles of his private philosophy. His sympathy for guerrilla herdsmen, their courage and conviction, illumines his own academic vendettas. A venomous wit made enemies of those with whom his disagreement went to a deep personal level where loyalty and integrity were at issue.

The Sanusiya is an Islamic Brotherhood, an order of Sufis or Darwishes. Of Sufi mysticism, Evans-Pritchard wrote that it fills the need of simple people for warmth and color in religion and provides personal contact and tenderness in the cult of saints.

> In every religion there will be found people who, like the Sufis, feel that while final acceptance of the tenets of the faith and conscientious performance of its duties are sufficient for righteousness and salvation, they do not satisfy the deeper longings of the soul which seeks always by entire love of God a perfect communion with Him. Human souls are rays of the divine sun imprisoned in the material world of the senses. The aim of Sufism has been to transcend the senses and to attain through love identification with God so complete that there is no longer a duality of "God" and "I," but there is only "God."[15]

Asceticism, isolation, contemplation, charity, and religious exercises producing a state of ecstasy charac-

[15] *The Sanusi of Cyrenaica*, p. 2.

terized the Sufi way of life. However, the Bedouin of Cyrenaica, among whom the Sanusiya Brotherhood was established in 1843, were not given to demonstrative, still less to ecstatic forms of worship. It was "difficult to imagine them piercing their cheeks with skewers, eating glass or swaying into convulsions." Moreover, they had only the slightest knowledge of the Sanusi teachings or ritual. Evans-Pritchard addressed his book to explaining the historic association between these thoroughly pragmatic people and their learned and spiritual leaders.

The answer partly lies in the lineage structure of Bedouin internal rivalries. The Bedouin welcomed independent arbitration and the immigrant tribes and their saintly lineages were glad to provide it (an anthropological approach). The rest of the answer lies in the pressures of Italian colonialism and war (a historical approach). The personalities of Sanusi leaders fused with the fiery independence and physical endurance of Bedouin herdsmen. Evans-Pritchard's book, which has been deeply influential among students of Arab civilization, can be seen as his second manifesto, or guideline. It affirms the power of personal interventions in historical events. In this respect it carries the spirit of his postwar writing as clearly as the Egyptian lectures had outlined his early program of research.

Accountability among the Azande

V

The anthropologist is forced by fieldwork not to
treat words apart from actions because in situations being observed the words so often have a
specific performative role. The words have the
same effect as an action. Austin[1] mentions the
placing of bets and the naming of ships as examples of words which, once spoken, permanently
alter a situation. Writing similarly of words,
Aaron Cicourel insists that all speech, not just the
ritually distinctive forms, have a constitutive
function.[2] The policeman's warning, "Anything
you say now may be taken down and used as evidence against you," no more than the host's form
of greeting and farewell, and the guest's mur-
murs of appreciation, constitutes an event as one
of a particular kind. Because of the words, the

[1] J. L. Austin, *How to Do Things with Words.*
[2] A. Cicourel, *Cognitive Sociology,* p. 112.

things that have happened are classed in certain ways, entailing certain consequences that would not have followed if such speeches had not been uttered. If this is true at all times, how much more striking are the declaratory, performative, and constitutive aspects of speech when the words are magic spells. There we go— immediately plunged into the problem of defining magic. But Evans-Pritchard obviated it by recognizing one world of existences (that assumed by logico-experimental scientific thought of his own day) and being prepared to find other worlds with different being and powers, justified by other assumptions locked into other institutional commitments. By declaring his own epistemological stand he could observe the other games.

The Azande put their most anxious problems to their poison oracle. Consulting the oracle, Evans-Pritchard tells us, involves feeding the poison to a chicken and addressing it clearly in words. The poison is told to kill the chicken if the answer is Yes; the second time around for the same question it is told to kill the chicken if the answer is No. Evidently the poison can understand, it acts intelligently, but it must obey; it has no discretion to reveal or hide the truth, no will; it is not a person or any kind of spiritual being, only a delicate piece of technology. The oracle is vulnerable to certain contaminations, but unerring in its answers if properly protected and approached. There is no little person hidden inside the poison; the Azande deride the idea that just because it can answer questions it might be a person, as an example of British simplicity. But all oracles by their function have to be able to understand. That this one is addressed in words does not raise more of a problem about Azande credulity than an oracle addressed with bones or tea leaves. Precise speech is necessary in this case because the consulter wants to know who is bewitching his affairs. To put the names correctly, in order of plausibility as potentially malevolent persons, is a necessary part of the action. But the speech, however precise, is only a small part of the consultation. To get the full meaning, the anthropologist has to track all the pathways of possible action against a rival or unfriendly neighbor. In the end (and there tends to be an end) the oracle enables someone to be held accountable. The evidence for the anthropologist includes what the Azande say and also what they do. They hold each other accountable and their tracing of accountability does not stop even after the arbitration of death.

The question of magic has decisively shifted: the anthropologist is not wondering whether to classify the people as animistic or preanimistic, magical or religious. The matter of slotting their beliefs into prearranged categories is not at issue. The question is what sustains Azande beliefs in oracles, what gives the oracles credibility in the first place? The answer is the same as for any system of beliefs: an array of fundamental assumptions that are never visible to the people who make them. Evans-Pritchard was sure that these capable craftsmen and farmers were not unduly swayed by emotions and that none of the then-current psychological theories about magic would fit their case. In his Egyptian lectures, he described the sociological approach to belief that he intended to develop.

This is how his explanation goes: The Azande could not live in the complex society they developed if their understanding of cause and effect were not the same as everyone else's. With most mishaps, they can say precisely what was the cause, whether technical incompetence or the interference of a powerful politician. But there is an area for curiosity that they pursue to the depths, though we Westerners leave it unplumbed. That is the ego-focused question of why any particular mishap should fall on *me* particularly. Why should two causal sequences converge so that I should happen to be in the hunting party and be in the way when the buffalo turns to gore? Why should I eat bananas every day and today eat one that disagrees with me? Why should the crumbling roof of the granary, bound to collapse one day, collapse on the day that my exposed head is there taking shade? This range of curiosity about the intersection of chains of events with my personal life is met in Azande culture by a set of pre-pared answers and actions. The most likely explanation is generally witchcraft. The right procedure is to con-sult an oracle to discover the name of the witch and then go to the accused and ask him to stop. Azande curiosity is roused (while ours is not) by the "Why me?" question because for them it unlocks a series of institutionalized procedures by which they hold each other accountable. We have other institutions which direct curiosity dif-ferently.

The Azande were deeply preoccupied with witchcraft, but one could not say they were dominated by witchcraft fears. Witchcraft was an ordinary, everyday part of their lives. An Azande would feel the same indignation on learning that a neighbor was bewitching his affairs as we might feel on learning that a colleague had been caught embezzling. The keynote, as it were, of their system of accountability is the assumption that anyone around might deserve to be blamed for any misfortune.

So long as the offense was a minor one and could be checked, the witchcraft belief-institution had a lubricat-ing effect on community life. Grudges would not be al-lowed to fester. To discover that a neighbor suspected you of harming his crops or his children was a warning to be specially considerate and polite to him. The stereotype of a witch was of a miserly, unmannerly, greedy person. To

deflect accusations, the Azande developed a high standard of courtesy. There was sufficient confidence in the
oracle and in the neighbors to believe that a witch publicly accused was a witch stopped. Consequently next
time trouble arose, or if trouble did not instantly abate,
the same name would not be proposed to the oracle again.
Through a prolonged series of disasters a man might confront every person he had ever quarreled with, one by
one, and ask him to desist. This was not at all the same
as asking for forgiveness. The accuser had very likely
quarreled with the accused in the past, but the oracle
showed the latter to be the aggressor. The accused person
was expected to perform a blessing. Goodwill would be
restored, the air was cleared, and social life would go on.

For such beliefs to work smoothly some secondary
elaborations were developed in the theory. An inherited
physical substance in the body was thought to be the
seat of witchcraft. A person could have it in a mild way;
or it could grow powerful and so dominate his emotions
that he could not keep cool control of his envy and spite.
A man was more likely to be a witch than a woman. Children and young persons were more likely to be victims
than attackers. The older a man grew, the stronger and
more dangerous his witchcraft. This elaboration elim-
inated minors from the roster of plausible names of people to be held accountable. It is more plausible that a
successful person be attacked by envious peers.

Another elaboration made it possible to accuse without
causing more enmity all around. A witch could act un-
consciously. This allowed a person accused by a neighbor
of viciously spoiling crops or making children ill to express concerned surprise: rather like, "My dear fellow,
I had no idea, how dreadful . . . I am so sorry. Hey,
bring the water for the blessing, I will keep a close watch
so this does not happen again." There was little ignominy

in being accused: on the contrary, since any man was likely to have witchcraft, one was grateful to be warned, as if one had a dangerous dog or a smoking chimney. At this level of accounting for minor misfortunes, the beliefs were a way of facilitating neighborly good relations, or at least a damper on possible explosions.

However, major misfortunes must sometimes occur. Witchcraft theory also explained death and permitted vengeance. A witch who had killed was a public danger, and the kin of this witch were expected to attend to his execution. In the old days (before the Anglo-Egyptian Condominium had forbidden it), a poison ordeal, administered to the accused instead of to a chicken, detected and killed the guilty witch. The poison ordeal was administered, as a branch of the judiciary, by the prince. Some people could come through the ordeal unharmed, others succumbed. The death of witches in the ordeal upheld the belief in witchcraft and in the efficacy of the ordeal. Moreover, the social demands for justice and vengeance were satisfied. If the suspect could not be brought to drink the poison, the prince's oracle would confirm (by poison given to chickens) whether he was indeed guilty and if so, gave permission for the victim's kin to spear him. At one level this would seem to be the end of the matter. But it is not the end of possible action and further justification to which the system of belief is put. The anthropologist's inquiry goes on.

At this stage of analysis, Evans-Pritchard had shown how the local institutions were integrated with central political authority. The oracle was presented as an instrument of political control. But the Azande were highly intelligent, critical, and skeptical people. A person accused and judged guilty did not necessarily accept the verdict, nor did his kin. It might be extremely inconvenient to do so. The Azande were continually testing and trying to

verify their oracle. For example, according to their theory, witchcraft was inherited in the male line. If a man
were speared as a witch, his sons would be proven to be
genetically tainted. Their chance of rebutting accusations
made against themselves would be better if they could
show their father to have been falsely accused and un-
justly killed. Evans-Pritchard now had other institutions
to explain: the autopsy on the body of a convicted witch.
It would be the honorable duty of a dear friend of the de-
ceased to make the lateral gash in his side and to unwind
his intestines on a forked stick to be inspected by a team
of experts. The experts might well declare that witchcraft
substance was absent, in which case the mourners would
have cleared the name of their family and have a claim to
compensation. But the failure of the oracles would need
to be explained. Not much problem about that. Oracles
were very delicate pieces of machinery, very sensitive to
contamination; any little carelessness in protecting the
poison or in purifying the oracle-consulter would explain
a mistake. Fortunately the prince had a nearly infallible
oracle. No ruler could expect to keep three hundred wives
and political hegemony without an efficient intelligence
system. Only the prince had both the incentive and the
means to protect the purity of his oracle. So every one
had an incentive to bring problems to the princely oracle.
The connection between the local witchcraft idea-institu-
tion and the centralized power supported the whole society. All the prince needed to do to control awkward
questions was to enforce secrecy about the results of the
oracle consultations.

In two pages I have summarized a system whose philosophical implications Evans-Pritchard elaborates over
five hundred pages. Everything works: each part contributes to the maintenance of the whole; no engines are
idling. The work that the thought does is social. After this

study was published, it should not have been possible to make philosophical statements about thought without recognizing that thought makes cuts and connections between actions. Questions about rationality should be questions about the coherence of particular actions within articulated institutions.

At the time that Evans-Pritchard was there, Azande society had undergone radical change. The princes were no longer supreme and autonomous; their wars had stopped and their armies were disbanded. Only a semblance of their former lives remained: their motives, risks, and rewards were now set at a low level by the Anglo-Egyptian Condominium. Consequently the theory and practice of witchcraft also had been adapted to new conditions. To accuse a person of witchcraft in a colonial court was forbidden, to kill a witch was a capital offense: no more poisoning and no more spearing.

The system of ideas might have changed more than it did had not the princes, still in control, made a minor adaptation of past practice. In any princedom, the prince's oracle now gave poison to chickens instead of to people. It had always been the infallible oracle; it was no change to bring all accusations of lethal witchcraft to court to be confirmed or rejected. It had always been *lèse majesté* to reveal the results of the prince's oracle, an offense punishable by death. Very likely it had always been the custom when asking whether a kinsman died as a victim of witchcraft to make an outward show of his innocence, whatever the prince's verdict. One would go into public mourning for the full period prescribed for an innocent death, whether it had been declared innocent or guilty; one would come out of mourning as if cleansed by the rituals and avenged by the execution of the witch. Now, instead of sometimes spearing him and sometimes poisoning the witch, the only recourse was to kill by secret magic. In the old days the corpse of the witch was proof that vengeance had been done, but now that part was more tricky.

There were gaps in the institutions which a theory of vengeance magic filled. Even if the poison oracle had ruled him not an innocent victim but a witch justly killed by vengeance magic, the kin of a dead man would start an elaborate parade of his innocence. They would go to a vendor of magic, pay for it to seek out their alleged enemy, and dispatch him. The magic was detective, judge of witchcraft, and executioner. The mourners would wait, scanning news of deaths in the neighborhood, not so unreasonable as to expect their magic to act at once, but eventually consulting their oracles as to whether the latest death could be claimed by the magic they had bought. Of course they would never reveal what they had done. A dark area of institutions in which no questions could be asked or knowledge revealed kept the old system functioning—exactly as Bartlett had foreseen.

Evans-Pritchard discovered this occluded area when he worked out that if the causes of deaths were added up, everyone would be claiming to be an innocent victim of witchcraft; at the same time, since every victim was also reckoned to have been avenged, the deaths from vengeance should have come near to equalizing the deaths of victims. Here was a discrepancy that struck the outsider but never worried the Azande. They could follow up any line of reasoning that had implications for action: if no action were entailed, there was no curiosity or incentive to probe further. The institutions themselves were precariously held together by fictions: the princes were no longer real princes, their status had little power. The same paste and paper that covered the cracks in the political system covered cracks in the thought system. At this stage Evans-Pritchard took a natural-history ap-

proach. He worked out the taxonomy and traced the connection between the parts. But for this exercise, he would
have been unable to observe a discrepancy of which in-
siders did not need to take note. Nor would he have been
able to validate his insight that magic, like other thinking, is a vehicle of social concerns, its logic limited only
by the limits of socially recognized responsibility.

The Azande had a genetic theory of witchcraft transmission. The theory was adapted so that questions about
transmission were directed away from those social relationships where claims could not be collected. If witchcraft went in the male line, then it would be unwise for
a son to accuse his father or a father his son, for either
would imply a tainted heredity for the accuser; moreover, there was no way either could get compensation of
any kind or from the other.

The situation is very comparable to the inhibitions
against exploring genetic transmission of intelligence in
our own society. Liberal thinkers back out of this possible
inquiry in horror of dubbing any part of the human race
congenitally superior or inferior. It is also worth dodging
such inquiry: political embarrassment inhibits it, for anyone who boldly raises the question may have awkward
criticism to meet about the illiberality of his views.

So when Evans-Pritchard asked the Azande how it was
that everyone did not have witchcraft in their genetic
makeup, since all were intermarried, they were surprised.
It seemed not to have occurred to them that it was incon-
sistent to go through the elaborate autopsy to clear a dead
man's name and to declare one particular descent line to
be clear, when by their own theory all must be equally
tainted. It is not illogical of them. They had riders to the
main hypothesis, which could explain why a particular
person was not a witch even if his lineage was known to
be a witch line. But more practically, there was much to

be gained by foregrounding the genetic theory on some occasions and ignoring it on others. Thus the interlocking of institutions produces blocks to inquiry.

On the other hand, because they made witchcraft accusations, a theory of consciousness had to be elaborated in Azande thought. Other peoples who believe in witchcraft have other prophylactic measures and ways of dealing with it without naming the suspect. They often think it fatal to mention the name of a person believed to be bewitching their affairs, lest the gossip makes the suspect angry enough to kill. In such a situation, if the witch is not going to be publicly accused, they can live comfortably with the idea that the witch is a fully conscious agent. But since the whole apparatus of Azande institutions for dealing with witches involved asking them to stay their dangerous actions, the institution of public accusation was made easier by the theory of unconscious witchcraft.

Then again, the theory of witchcraft, being essentially a method of pinning blame on others, had to be tailored to fit the social requirements for proper moral and technical responsibility. Individuals were held accountable in Azande society for their technical incompetence. It availed a bad craftsman nothing to claim that a witch made his tools slip. To blame witchcraft for a bad technical performance would only arouse laughter. And the same for moral responsibility: it availed an adulterer nothing to protest to the injured husband that a witch caused him to commit adultery; of course not, the Azande were too clever. One system of complaints and claims was separated from another until the area in which witchcraft was an allowable charge against someone was fully defined: it was the area of ambiguous relationships, rivalries between peers, points in their institutions where friction arises and where no buffers of social rank or wealth created distance between persons. And even in that area, the kind of disasters that could be charged to witches were limited so as not to drain personal responsibility out of the system. Here again we can talk of a system of accountability, because its boundaries are clear. All deaths except for those in war were attributed to witchcraft; it would be hopeless to pursue claims against witches behind the enemy lines, and so here the accountability system stopped again.

The complementary aspects of different kinds of claims are apparent when we find that no members of the aristocratic clan could ever be accused of witchcraft, because of an axiomatic belief that there was no witchcraft in their line of descent. This hereditary cutoff insured that commoners would not tangle with aristocrats by accusing them of witchcraft. It also insured that aristocrats did not accuse one another. But since their lives were full of opportunities for hatred and jealousy another theory explained how they could do comparable harm to each other: aristocrats used sorcery, spells, and magic, material substances to harm, even if they were not endowed with the witch's innate psychic powers.

When this analysis is complete, there appear to be gaps in the Azande thought system, but the institutions are integrated. The gaps in the thinking sustain the interdigitation of the institutions. Whenever there is a pressure to introduce order into social behavior, regulatory ideas develop, but each set of regulations as it gets applied creates other areas where uncertainty needs to be reduced. To make the institutions work, new ideas are produced to fit the pieces coherently together or to sustain the credibility of the whole. The institutions are an abstraction; they have no life of their own; the pressure to organize thought introduces new entities into the universe, such as hereditary witchcraft substance in the intestines, or careful distinctions between witchcraft and nonhereditary powers of sorcery. The special Azande array of existences unknown to our world all derive from concerns to escape accountability or to hold people to account.

Naturally each Azande was more specially interested in the possibilities of holding other people accountable than in being held to account. They were bent on arguing that they and their kin were victims and their neighbors were aggressors. Their thought was dominated more by suspicion than by trust. The Nuer, by contrast, appeared to be more occupied by the conditions for sustaining a system of self-help; that is, by a concern to insure that kin delivered reciprocal support. The two kinds of concern went with two different qualities in person-to-person dealings. One kind of social reality, built on one kind of accountability, invested fellow humans with sinister psychic powers; the other subjected a world filled with spirits and ghosts to the will of a righteous god.

Evans-Pritchard's exercise in understanding Azande witchcraft beliefs has resounding implications for philosophy. But though the Azande are as much quoted[3] as the Bororo, one suspects that *Witchcraft, Oracles, and Magic among the Azande* is not frequently read. We, in our culture, have endowed only a particular set of existences with plausibility. One of the sources of error lies in the assumption that the universes of other cultures should hold no more and no less than the entities that interest ourselves. We should admit that we freely create new entities at need—for example, IQ, to solve social problems of competitive entry, or to absolve from legal responsibility. If we recognize that these entities are pat-

[3] M. Polanyi, *Personal Knowledge*, pp. 287–94; P. Winch, "Understanding a Primitive Society"; H. F. Pitkin, *Wittgenstein and Justice*, pp. 247–50.

ently devised as part of our system of accountability, and that there are as many opaque areas and gaps in our curiosity about them as the Azande have about their witches and demons, then Evans-Pritchard's lesson will have struck home.

Here we may pose a recurring question of sociological method and objectivity. Imported assumptions distort the interpretation of evidence. It is not difficult to make objectively valid statements about the Azande government. The role of prince is physically defined by habitation and clothing, as well as by the pattern of footsteps on the ground. But when it comes to their ideas about witchcraft, one has to be careful. It is legitimate to ask how Azande witchcraft ideas intermesh with Azande political ideas, and how Azande witchcraft institutions relate to Azande political institutions, however these may be consistently defined. But to ask how these ideas in general affect institutions implies that the ideas have a life of their own and can be observed influencing the institutions—whereas, in all cases, it is people who have ideas and who influence institutions. An expectation that ideas can somehow be mapped out apart from the institutions in which they work is similarly misleading. Again, to present the general relation between ideas and institutions as a feasible field of inquiry—leaving out the persons and intentions that generate both—is another form of the fallacy. It is as if a neurologist were to claim to investigate mind and matter, when all he is capable of doing is tracing which parts of the brain control which neural systems, always recognizing that this alleged brain control is proved by particular movements in the body.

The larger overview is necessary, of course, and should be undertaken by everyone, all the time, and not only by qualified metaphysicians. Sherrington conducted this generalizing exercise when he wrote a popular and highly influential book on *Man on His Nature* (1953). The general inquiry of where we are now should not be shirked. But it should be conducted, as Sherrington conducted his, within a frankly metaphysical frame of reference. Within the authoritative framework of sociological inquiry, the arbitrary separating of ideas from the institutions in which they work creates a pernicious dichotomy, as if mind were out there, an existence, disembodied, supported by nothing, but somehow powerfully influencing the solidly physical institutions in curious ways. This perspective allows insoluble questions to fill the central forum of sociological debate.

Accountability among the Nuer

vi

The fieldwork remove from Azande to Nuer forced
an extraordinary awareness on Evans-Pritchard.
He was already very sensitive to methodological
problems. Working through the magical beliefs of
the Azande and coming out the other side with a
full account of their rationality, through correct
chains of inference to the underlying assumptions and from these to their plausibility as em-
bodied in social institutions, he was alert to the
pitfalls. Before he published *Witchcraft, Oracles,
and Magic among the Azande* in 1937, he had already finished his Nuer fieldwork. The two intense experiences lived side by side in his mind
while he wrote the first book.

It is possible to describe Azande institutional
life and the distribution of power and, in discussing their system of thought, to map the parts
of each upon the other. Rudimentary in some

cases and hypertrophied in others, their social institutions can be transposed to our own view of the main divisions of social life; the family, local government, judiciary, military, and governmental functions had their obvious distinctive counterparts. Not so with the Nuer. The style of Nuer life at once reveals the local limitations of our categories. Their institutions are invisible. Every now and again a regulatory idea surfaces and marshals activity, then sinks out of sight, while another becomes visible in its effect upon movements of cattle and people. If they can be said to have anything corresponding to political institutions, these have absolutely no physical form, no architecture of palaces or prisons, no embodiment in piles of stones—not even any territorial divisions except those made by natural features such as rivers, watering little communities separated by drier land from the others. Even the verbal grading of different sociological levels is absent: the Nuer word for lineage is used at every level, so that the biggest tribe and all its constituent units are called by the same term. Anyone already alert to false abstractions and careless imposing of ideas from one culture to another would meet here the perfect challenge to make a new beginning.

We should distinguish two senses in which the word "system" is used in the social sciences. The commonsense use of system refers to a set of relationships such that all parts contribute to the maintenance of the whole. If one element is changed, then because of their systematic connection all will be transformed. The main interest here is the taxonomic interconnections. A tribe undergoing industrial/colonial pressures may start to grow cash crops; the task of the anthropologist examining the social system is to trace how the one or two changes in technology affect the economy, family, life, religion, and so on. At this rather simple level of theory, it is usual to assume that something about the interrelation of the parts insures also that when one element is altered, there is still some power to return to the original pattern, a homeostatic assumption. It makes sense to assert that a principle of stability must be there if the society seems to endure minor changes and resist major ones. But saying that there is homeostasis is not to explain how it works.

The other usage of the word system focuses directly upon homeostatic principles. The work of the investigator is to identify how the stabilizing controls work. Norbert Wiener, who has already appeared in this book as the young man who gave Frederick Bartlett an idea about how to experiment with memory, founded the branch of science called cybernetics; a cybernetic control mechanism is one in which the system's inputs turn themselves off, and on again, so that a given state is maintained at the level set by the controls. The thermostatic oven is a familiar example. Wiener developed his idea to explain how living organisms maintain a regular body temperature; he also applied it to many other systems.

Evans-Pritchard presented the Nuer political system in terms of feedback. He described the inputs and the regulatory mechanism; the output was the political system maintained at a certain level of assured safety for life, limb, and property. He worked out the model because there was nothing else to use from existing political theory or anthropology to explain an ordered society kept in being without the exercise of centralized, coercive power.

The Azande political stage was filled with princes, governors, deputies, aristocrats and commoners, mutilated convicts, rich men, poor men, and many other social statuses that can be mapped onto territorial fields of responsibility. But the Nuer political scene is sparse, practically empty.

The social life of the Nuer is strongly regulated. Every man knows what is due to him. A tally of compensation for insults and injuries is known, any transaction in rights is affirmed by a corresponding transfer of livestock. If a debtor fails to pay, his creditor can walk into a strange camp, unhitch a beast of corresponding value, and safely walk away with it, no friends of the debtor lifting a finger to harm or stop him. Regulation is there, but power is diffused through the whole system. Each man has to defend his own rights.

Many other tribes are organized on principles that seem to be something of this self-help kind, but when there is really a free-for-all, the strongest wins, and contests of individual strength are daily events. The elementary principle of self-help usually produces great disparities of wealth and power. But here, with the Nuer, the strongest does not win. There is little accumulation of wealth. The cattle, goats, and sheep are evenly distributed among households. There is no accumulation of power. The phrase ordered anarchy seems to describe the situation. There is no social contract, no agreement to limit individual liberties so as to allow power to accumulate with one or two people for the sake of the good order.

The regulation has to be analyzed at three levels: first, the diffusion of power over balanced segments of the tribe; second, the maintenance of the balance; third, the thought system that values each individual self and makes a frame by which self can be transcended. Only this third analysis reveals the switch control for the political feedback system.

The phrase structural opposition summarizes the system by which power is diffused throughout the Nuer tribe. All the units of the society are divided according to clearly known orders of magnitude. At the highest level, the whole tribe divides into two or possibly three sections; then each of these divides again, and these again and again, until the smallest political units, the local communities, are reached. The local neighborhoods, containing several villages, are usually self-sufficient in seasonal resources. Within a village everyone counts as kin. At the next inclusive level, within a local community, there is a sense of common interest, more quarreling and sharing, than between communities. A quarrel with people in far-distant communities is less likely, for the more people have to do with each other, the more cause there is for quarreling. When a Nuer feels insulted or wronged, he does not take advice or seek arbitration.

He at once challenges the man who has wronged him to a duel and the challenge must be accepted. There is no other way of settling a dispute and a man's courage is his only protection against aggression. . . . From their earliest years children are encouraged by their elders to settle all disputes by fighting, and they grow up to regard skill in fighting the most necessary accomplishment and courage the highest virtue.

Boys will fight with spiked bracelets. Men of the same village or camp fight with clubs, for it is a convention that spears must not be used between close neighbours lest one of them be killed and the community be split by a blood-feud. It is also a convention that no third person may take part in the fight, even though he be a close kinsman of one of the combatants. Once a fight has begun neither party can give way and they have to continue till one or the other is badly injured unless, as generally happens, people pull them away from each other, loudly protesting, and then stand between them.

When a fight starts between persons of different villages it is with the spear; every adult male of both communities takes part in it; and it cannot be stopped before considerable loss of life has ensued. Nuer know this and, unless they are very angry, are reluctant to start a fight with a neighbouring village.[1]

[1] *The Nuer*, pp. 151–52.

This first superficial stage of Evans-Pritchard's analysis reveals the lines of cleavage along which Nuer hostilities flare up and are damped. The tribe is divided into segments, each of which has many characteristics of the tribe itself:

> Each has its distinctive name, its common sentiment, and its unique territory . . . so that the spatial divisions of the rains are maintained and may be accentuated during the drought. . . . The smaller the tribal segment, the more compact its territory, the more contiguous its members, the more varied and intimate their social ties, and the stronger therefore its sentiment of unity. . . .[2]

The first elementary principle of their organization is that political cohesion varies with variations of political distance and is also a function of structural distance in genealogical terms. The second is that each segment is further segmented. The third is that there is opposition between all the segmented parts. Members of any segment unite for wars against adjacent segments of the same order and unite with these adjacent segments against larger sections. These principles combine to make a political system founded upon the structural opposition of its parts. Every status and claim to loyalty is relative to the whole: at any point in time, the structural distance between opponents determines the constellation of enemies and allies, and this can change at any other point in time. At one time a small unit splits, at another time it fuses with its opponent against a larger foe. The continuous fission and fusion follows the predictable lines of structural distance. Evans-Pritchard had to call it structural distance, because though it has a geographical basis, geography does not fully describe its mobilizing effects, and though it has a connection with kinship, kinship does not explain how the land is divided up.

[2] Ibid., p. 142.

Hints of Einsteinian relativism color Evans-Pritchard's language here, and more than a hint of biological analogy. We should recall Sherrington's principle of reciprocal opposition and reinforcement in the nervous system. This Nuer political system is described by Evans-Pritchard as if the segments were moved by muscles that had power mutually to support or inhibit:

> Feuds are settled with comparative ease in a restricted social milieu where the structural distance between the participants is narrow, but they are more difficult to settle as the milieu expands, until one reaches the inter-tribal boundaries, where no compensation is offered or expected. The degree of social control over feuds varies with the size of the tribal segment, and Nuer themselves have often tried to explain this to me.[3]

The boundaries of the system are determined by the boundaries of the intention to treat all Nuer by the same rules. The force of law is not the same for all Nuer, but weakens with the structural distance between parties to a dispute. At the outer edges the will to deal justly with all Nuer, even if it were there, is checked by natural obstacles, physical distance, empty bushland, and the need to travel.

> The larger the segment involved the greater the anarchy that prevails. People say that there is payment of blood-cattle between primary sections, but they do not greatly feel the need of paying it. The tribe is the last stage in this increasing anarchy. It still has nominal unity. . . . If many men are killed in a big fight between large sections, nothing is done to avenge them or pay compensation for their deaths. Their kinsmen bide their time until there is another fight. The political integument may in consequence be stretched eventually to the breaking-point and the tribe split into two.[4]

[3] Ibid., p. 157.
[4] Ibid., pp. 157–58.

The second general characteristic of the Nuer political system is that its boundaries are created by logistic failure, not by foreign treaty. Political will and the rule of law just fade out at the edges of the system. For the Nuer, the boundaries of their system are the natural limits of law and order. Furthermore, in the sociology of knowledge to which their example contributes, the boundaries of their polity are the limits of their knowledge. The fact that there is a known boundary enables their thought to reach out to the edges, and move back in curling waves of analogy, folding one situation upon another, so that the match of metaphors is irresistible. By knowing how their social system is bounded they bound the possibilities of their knowledge system. Then they establish truth and understanding within it by innumerable proofs and demonstrations.

So much for the first point, the diffusion of power by structural opposition; Evans-Pritchard has not yet given any account of the principles of self-regulation, only a very convincing account of balance achieved through countervailing forces. Even at this stage it sounds seductively complete; one is tempted to be satisfied here, and not to ask how the opposing units in the Nuer structure are so well marked that balance is sustained, or to ask whether this is really the case or whether some other mechanism still needs to be uncovered. One might mention that most anthropologists, in describing a political system, bring their own inquiry to rest when they have shown a balance of forces.

At the next stage of questioning, Evans-Pritchard described the feedbacks. The inputs to the political system are the obligation to fight and the principle of descent through males that aligns real or fictive brothers, but forbids brothers (as situationally defined) to fight against each other. The control mechanism combines the feud, the possibility of paying blood compensation instead of taking a life for a life, and the theory that homicide pollutes the earth. No honorable man would accept cattle in place of a slain brother, but human bloodshed pollutes the earth, so that whole communities are endangered: if the kin of the slayer were to drink or eat with the kin of the victim, they would all die from the contamination of blood. Nothing would save them except religious sacrifice to wipe out the pollution. The effect of this theory is to bring great pressure to bear upon disputing parties if they live in the same village or even in the same neighborhood, for all the people who drink the same river water are placed at risk, all being kin to one or both parties. The fear of pollution of blood fades out beyond the local community and is totally ineffective where structural and geographical distances decrease the risks of shared water resources. The pollution theory is nicely adjusted to political realities. It gives the local doves some leverage against the hawks, obliging them to swallow their pride, accept forty head of cattle (no mean amount), and save the community from epidemic.

Insofar as a feud cannot be settled peacefully between distant segments, each new outbreak of killing defines the lines between them—a Durkheimian point. Insofar as blood-pollution theory brings truce and peace, it does so in the places where kinship and local loyalties are strong. The theory is credible because it fits the institutions. The feud maintains the structural opposition, defines the units, identifies the areas of lasting solidarity. Each time the internal opposition by which the system maintains itself rises to the point of blood being shed, the latent hostility within the smallest units is damped by pollution fears. "The likelihood of a homicide developing into a blood-feud, its force, and its chances of settlement are thus dependent on the structural interrelations of the persons concerned."[5]

To complete the analysis, the anthropologist has to delve further into the thought system that channels personal pride to the defense of political boundaries. Nuer pride reaches extraordinary heights.

> The ordered anarchy in which they live accords well with their character, for it is impossible to live among Nuer and conceive of rulers ruling over them. The Nuer is a product of hard and egalitarian upbringing, is deeply democratic, and is easily roused to violence. His turbulent spirit finds any restraint irksome and no man recognizes a superior. . . . That every Nuer considers himself as good as his neighbour is evident in their every movement. They strut about like lords of the earth, which, indeed, they consider themselves to be. There is no master and no servant in their society, but only equals who regard themselves as God's noblest creation. Their respect for one another contrasts with their contempt for all other peoples. Among themselves even the suspicion of an order riles a man and either he does not carry it out or he carries it out in a casual and dilatory manner that is more insulting than a refusal.[6]

Why is pollution of blood such a fearful thing to the Nuer that it can constrain their pride and end a feud? The Nuer hold themselves in a tension of pride and humility: the pride is in their superiority to every other person, the humility in their habit of reflecting deeply on the human condition and on their relation to God. The relativity of their moral code continually places them in ambiguous and conflicting situations. They must fight, they must not shed blood: this is an example of the moral knife-edge on which they continually walk, their

[5] Ibid., p. 158.
[6] Ibid., pp. 181–82.

daily lives hedged with rules that circumstances inevitably lead them to break. No wonder they say that a man
is bound to commit faults, that faults accumulate with
out the offender's being aware of what he has done. To
meet these double pulls of moral consciousness they have
worked out complex exonerations and remissions, with
fine distinctions between accidental and intentional
wrongdoing, faults graded from big to small. Keeping all
these reflections in suspense, to the advantage of clear
decision they gather them into a single strong theory of
God, sin, expiation, and forgiveness achieved by sacrifice. Pollution of the earth by bloodshed would hardly be
a credible danger if it did not figure on a list of many
other sins regularly seen to entail illness and death if not
expiated. Their commitment to a theory of sin and of its
consequences is the ontological anchorage for the control mechanism of Nuer political life. Equivalent to the
Azande of witchcraft, the Nuer theory of sin is the
touchstone of reality to which all their elaborate legal
fictions relate.

Some of the threads of Evans-Pritchard's argument
can now be drawn together. The foundation of meaning,
according to my reconstruction upon his work, is the system of accountability. As people decide to hold others accountable, and as they allow the same principles to extend universally, even to apply to themselves, they set up
a particular kind of moral environment for each other.
According to the pressures created by this environment
the mind's thought is discriminated and toughened. The
Nuer hold others totally accountable; they must be prepared to die and prepared to kill. They expect themselves
to be held equally accountable. The price is so high that
they notch up detailed tallies of mutual accountability
and split logical hairs with the gusto of medieval casuists,
to establish precise obligations. Their commitment to

their system of accountability gives them the incentive to work out the fullest exegesis of their principles. Surely no Talmudists excel the Nuer in establishing the string of consequences entailed by principles. For the anthropologist's purpose, they were even better fitted than the Azande to demonstrate the powers of hard reasoning active in primitive society.

Evans-Pritchard's fieldwork method required him to support everything he said with evidence drawn from observation, the evidence that would be squeezed out of greetings and quarrels and especially from reaction to misfortune. He tried never to declare a belief or theory not supported by action. The deed explains the principle as much as the principle explains the deed.

A test case arises with the word idiom, one of his favorite terms for discussing Nuer political organization. He calls a principle an idiom, when, although appealed to locally as if a description, it is in no way an accurate description of what is happening. The idiom of descent through the male line is a way of thinking about political relations; it provides a conceptual framework for political organization; it is a way of thinking about the relation between political units "as though"[7] it were a relation between kinsmen, *as though* the tribe were a genealogical system, *as though* the local community were identical with a lineage it was named after. Usually, when idiom or ideology is used to explain social behavior, no other explanation is available. The idiom, instead of being merely a local medium of description, is treated as an explanation in itself.

Why do they do this or this? For ideological reasons or because they think in this idiom.[8] When Evans-Pritchard

[7] Ibid., p. 229.
[8] Ibid., pp. 205, 211, 212, 228, 229, 236; *Kinship and Marriage among the Nuer*, pp. 179, 180.

writes in this vein, is there not a falling off from the strict positivist ideal on which he assembles his evidence? Why can he not drop the idiom and say that the lineage is identical with the local community, and that the local communities are connected with each other by ties of male descent? He cannot, because it is not true. Nuer lineages are not corporate, localized communities. They are dispersed and mixed up together. His census did not produce any picture of a system of genealogical relationships connecting male relatives with each other and local units linked with each other, as descendants of brothers, or sons and fathers. The Nuer move freely over the land and settle where they please. The real units in the political system are villages and their local communities. This being so, any skeptic is at liberty to ask for the evidence of this alleged idiom of descent in the male line.

But Evans-Pritchard very carefully assembled evidence for the many shared commitments to legal fictions by which Nuer social life is maintained. Lineage has little reality as a residential unit; like other social institutions among the Nuer the lineage emerges at specific occasions, for example at sacrifices when its members travel a long way to be together. It emerges clearly at feasts and distributions of cattle. As a residential principle, no; as an active principle of organization for wealth holding the evidence is convincing that this idiom is more than a way of thinking about institutions, it is a way of organizing them within the local communities. Between community neighborhoods the idiom applies: the politics of fission and fusion among balanced segments work entirely through the categories of descent in the male line.

The political institutions of the Nuer have special interest for the sociology of knowledge. Their institutions successively and momentarily appear in their actions and disappear, leaving no physical traces. Political life never entails contributing to the upkeep of roads and bridges or paying a levy to a leader. They do not build a court-house or even a pillory. This is part of the extraordinary attraction of these people: whatever political principles exist are maintained entirely in their minds. The feed-back of the political system works within the system of thought. Nuer hold each other accountable according to ideas of lineage affiliation. They have certain clear ideas about what it is to be in the right, and they agree that most Nuer are most of the time at fault. Somewhere in their ideas about what can go wrong and how to set it right, a whole social system is evolved, negative feed-backs and all.

The model is well enough explained. If it be correctly understood, it can illuminate a central problem in phi-losophy. That thought is embedded in institutions has been established. Now it is a matter of asking what kinds of thoughts and what kinds of institutions. From this ex-ample we can compare accountability systems to offer fresh answers to the old questions. From here on I shall assume that whatever can be said about a belief as be-longing to a system implies the same about the relevant social institution, since each only lives in the other.

Reasoning and Memory

vii

Individuals vary greatly in their capacity to·recall past experiences. Once, psychologists treated memory as if it were an isolated faculty of the mind, of which the most conclusive tests would measure the capacity to retain and reproduce arbitrary strings of information.[1] It would take away from the high marks that could be scored to the credit of pure memory if the subject had some interest in the topic or if the items made some sort of sense to him. Against this trend of experimental work, which was not producing impressive results, Bartlett had entered the contrary idea that memory is directly influenced by social factors. We have seen that he did not succeed in devising tests that would go beyond this affirmation. But when he wrote that social conditions

[1] F. C. Bartlett, *Thinking: An Experimental and Social Study,* pp. 142–44.

control individual recall "by providing that setting of interest, excitement and emotion which follows the development of specific images and socially by providing a
persistent framework of restrictions and customs which
acts as a schematic basis for constructive memory"[2] he
had wished to introduce a new approach to experimental
psychology.

Alas for Bartlett that he did not understand better what
Maurice Halbwachs was trying to do on the selfsame
subject. A pupil of Henri Bergson, of Durkheim, and of
Mauss, Halbwachs took for his main research project to
demonstrate that perception and recall depend primarily
upon social institutions and secondly upon physical, visible symbols.[3]

In Durkheim's theory of religion the totem is an em-
blem that serves by its physical existence to fix an otherwise fleeting, abstract idea. If it were not for this physical
existence as a point of reference, ideas about religion
would have no stability. Second, for Durkheim's theory,
religious ideas are particularly vulnerable to destabilizing
forces because they are second-remove ideas about another abstraction, society itself. They depend on social
commitment. Insofar as the individual has a commitment
to society, this commitment has to be hedged around
with physical markings, rules of taboo. The concept of
society as having overriding authority is transformed into
a concept of godhead.

Halbwachs's contribution is to work out in detail the
social and physical supports of memory. The temporal
stages of an event are more easily recalled if they can
be given a spatial ordering that corresponds to the temporal sequence. Concern to establish the social framework of memory leads him to discuss the different mem-

[2] F. C. Bartlett, *Remembering: A Study in Experimental and
Social Psychology*, p. 255.
[3] Halbwachs, *Les Cadres Sociaux de la Mémoire*.

ory of different social classes, pegged out by different physical memorials. Instead of considering the spatial layout of Australian camps or the seasonal movements of the Eskimos, as Durkheim and Mauss had done, he applied himself to European history and contemporary life. He was particularly interested in the negative case of how memory could be sustained without that spatial structure that seemed to be its prerequisite, in the same way as Durkheim had taught that religious organization has an inherent problem of cognitive stability unless it takes over a spatial anchorage.

Evans-Pritchard's work on reasoning and remembering derived from this double heritage: the English psychologist's interest in the institutional frameworks that sustain memory and the French sociologist's researches in the same direction. He presented Nuer social institutions as the schematic framework of memory. Whenever the Nuer seek to clarify the definition of a status, they state it in terms of claims to cattle. The intense emotional value of cattle in Nuer imagination and poetry should not be overlooked. Lines of relationships, so complex to the outsider to unravel, would be crystal clear and easy to recall to the person who stands to gain a cow or an ox from correctly computing them. Nuer social life illustrates how an individual's powers of retention and retrieval of information are stimulated by social factors. There are rewards for recognizing sharp distinctions and penalties for forgetting them. So keenness of individual perception is encouraged along prescribed lines. Memory will be continually revived by occasions on which claims would be contested and honored. Each wedding and funeral is an occasion for claims and counterclaims, to say nothing of the major crises of loyalty in fighting. Attention is strongly focused on distinctions used as principles for distributing wealth.

A set of questions arises about the social stimulus to

logical discrimination. How social life selectively focuses attention and jogs memory is important in itself. Just because attention is selective, gaps in knowledge inevitably appear. The Azande case illustrates institutionalized blocks to curiosity. The Nuer studies further illustrate principles of rejection that automatically send some information to oblivion. They also provide a complex example of benchmarks used to organize time past, by which historical series are grouped for retrieval. Since this work contributes to a central element in Marxist theory, that is the relation between superstructure and infrastructure, I am always surprised that self-styled Marxist anthropologists pay it so little attention—perhaps an institutional-ideological focus blocks curiosity.

First let me set the question of logical discrimination back into its old anthropological context. Recall that there are still extant societies that have no words for counting beyond the number three, and others in which four or seven is the limit of the numerate skills. Apparently people with no worldly possessions worth counting can manage quite comfortably with a linguistic competence for distinguishing numbers up to three only. Asked "How many of your children are living with you?" a mother with six around her knees will feel content to reply something like "a lot" or "many" or "all these." This does not mean she cannot name them all in order of birth or notice when one is missing. Judgment of quantities is an even more complex matter. Some shepherds are said to scan a large flock of sheep and register how many and which are absent in much less time than it would take to count them. However, a hundred years ago it was naturally tempting to consider these nonnumerates as simple children of nature, and to try to work out a social developmental sequence that paralleled that of the stages in which children learn to count. The implications of ranging such societies on a series from most infantile

to more numerate were never tested because extraordinary discrepancies in their capacities for reckoning, judgment, and memory rendered any single grading criterion
useless. Some people whose technology might cause them
to be placed at a primitive stage performed prodigious
feats of memory when it came to reciting genealogies of
kings or ancestors. The idea came to be accepted that
primitive people were good at learning by rote and that
their best remembering was the result of mechanical
mnemonics.

Bartlett thought that a strong social support to memory
was inclined to produce a mechanical style of recall. His
idea was that when the social institutions provided the
mnemonic setting, recall was of the recitative type; by
contrast, when an individual, free from the guidance and
constraints of his society, had to remember, he did so
with "none of that relatively effortless, recitative, copying
manner which marked the recall of the native. The plan
was built up bit by bit, a detail here, a filling up there,
then another key detail and so on. The whole process had
every appearance of a genuine construction."[4]

The idea that institutions are something which the
primitive takes as given—a fixed, unalterable part of his
environment—dies hard. It is one of the sources of a
theoretical division between ourselves, modern industrial
man, thought to be free of tradition's grip, free to argue
the toss and exert our influence over institutions, and
they, the primitives, who are supposed to accept the en-
crusted yoke of custom. Evans-Pritchard demonstrated
how they, too, negotiate their claims and construct their
culture in doing so. He did it by entering into the way
that the Nuer use their principles of discrimination.

In the perennial controversy about human behavior
and its psychological basis prohibitions on incest are

[4] F. C. Bartlett, *Remembering,* pp. 249–51.

often discussed. Sometimes it is argued that humans have a natural aversion to sexual congress with close kin, in which case the rules they observe are not intellectual constructions but instinctive responses. The counter-argument rests on the observation that humans are frequently not deterred by the alleged instinctive aversion: humans seem to be no different from animals in their readiness to mate with kin; and on this argument, social considerations explain the prevalence and form of such regulations. Nuer theory comes down unequivocally on the side of a sociological explanation of incest regulation. Nuer say that it is unthinkable for a mother and son to have sexual relations. The whole context for this unthinkability is laid out by their justification of the regulations in less heinous cases. Basically sex and marriage are organized by the transfer of cattle. Cattle-givers cannot give cattle to themselves, so the elementary requirements of a transaction draw a boundary around kin who hold common rights as cattle claimants. Every prohibited relationship is forbidden explicitly "because of the cattle." The regulation is on a par with our law which disallows evidence given in court by a wife against or for her husband.

Nuer incest regulations are as follows: marriage is forbidden between clansfolk—relationships traced in the male line. It is forbidden also between a man and a woman related through either father or mother (by male or female links) up to six generations. It is forbidden between close natural kinsfolk, that is, between persons related through sexual union outside of marriage; for example, a man could not marry the daughter of his maternal grandfather's natural son. Thus far the rules would seem to be concentrated on closeness of biological relationship, and might support the theory that an instinct is being codified into laws. But adoption is also a bar to intermarriage. A captured boy of the Dinka tribe, if adopted by his captors, counts as a son, and he cannot marry into their lineage. Even if he be adopted into a different lineage from that of his captors, men from his captor's lineage are forbidden to marry his daughter. The reason given is the same kind given in all cases: when the Dinka boy marries, his captors will contribute cattle to the marriage payments for his wife, which gives them a claim to some of the cattle that will come in when his daughter eventually marries; it is impossible for them to marry a girl at whose marriage they are entitled to claim cattle—it would be an incestuous union. The rule by which they forgo sex gives them a claim to the cows due to kinsfolk. Only if there were no recognized relationship can they have sexual intercourse or marry. When a captured Dinka girl is adopted, her adoptive kin perform a religious rite and say, "She will become our daughter and we will receive her bridewealth cattle." The cattle of her bridewealth give her kinship, and with it the right to receive the cows due to the paternal aunt on the marriage of her captor's sons. Marriage is forbidden between her descendants and the descendants of those kinsmen in virtue of her bridewealth for several generations. The Nuer state all the rules in terms of rights to cattle. The transfers of cattle create the close relationships that are incompatible with marriage.

The fact that a man cannot marry his wife's sister, or any near kinswoman of his wife, as second wife unless the first wife has died without children, is also explained in terms of cattle. "When your daughter is married her mother's sister is entitled to a cow of her bridewealth, and Nuer hold that she cannot both receive this cow and be your wife at the same time, especially as the cow is in some degree regarded as part of the bridewealth still owing from your marriage to your wife." The rules against marrying the daughter of an age-mate give an even clearer acknowledgment of the social nature of the prohibition.

> The blood age-mates have shed together into the ground at their initiation gives them a kind of kinship. In certain circumstances an age-mate may claim a cow . . . of the bridewealth of the daughter of one of his mates and a man may not be in the position of paying bridewealth and being able to claim it. Nuer point out also that were a man to marry the daughter of an age-mate her parents would become his parents-in-law, and the respect he would have to show them would be incompatible with the familiarity with which he should treat age-mates and their wives and the liberties he may take with them. He could not, for instance, eat and drink in their home, an abstention in glaring contradiction to the behavior expected of age-mates.[5]

Very evidently the Nuer divides his social universe into kin and not-kin. From male kin he expects support in fighting, vengeance if he is killed, and cattle distribution when kinswomen are married. Kinship means claims on cattle. Every wedding is an occasion for reviving memories of possible claims and so reviving the lines of relationship in people's minds.[6]

To state a claim on cattle is to divide the whole universe of possible relationships into two mutually exclusive spheres of claims: "Where the women are, the cattle are not." Either sex claims or cattle claims are possible, but both simultaneously are impossible.

If this does not begin to illustrate the relentless demands of social accountability upon logic, a further glance at Nuer marriage will convince. Nothing gives more zest to drawing fine logical distinctions than the need to distinguish among competing claims. But the desire to reconcile incompatible situations is another

[5] *The Nuer*, pp. 34–35.
[6] *Kinship and Marriage among the Nuer*, ch. II.

powerful stimulus to logical exercise. A person wants to hold, and yet to have the credit of giving away; to enjoy sexual adventures himself, while allowing no one to disrupt his own marriage; to let an unfaithful wife go away, but to claim all her offspring. Basically the Nuer want to have a social system in which rights are transmitted through wedlock, and at the same time not to constrain their womenfolk. Compared with Azande women, Nuer women enjoy great freedom and dignity. Nearly all the categories in the social system are generated through the marriage bond. Yet a Nuer woman is not forced to stay with a husband she dislikes. The Nuer reconcile potentially opposed patterns of behavior by a series of legal fictions. Starting from the principle that a legal marriage is established by the transfer of cattle, they pursue this principle through all the ramifications they desire.

Technically, so long as the cattle are not returned (and this is exceedingly difficult after they have been distributed to kin) a marriage endures. The mere fact that the husband dies does not end the marriage, for he has paid over the cattle once and for all. So with no new marriage being required, the widow should normally cohabit with one of his brothers. Any children begotten are still to be counted as the children of the dead man. What if she might not consent to live with any of the brothers of her late husband? The brothers whom she rejects do not try to force her to stay with them against her wishes. If she wants to go away and live with a man outside their group, she can, but the children she might bear to him are still legally the children of the man who paid for the cattle. If the natural father wants to legitimize his children, he only has to pay the appropriate amount of cattle. He has a material interest in doing so, for the payment entitles him to claim cows as a father at the marriage of his own daughters. If it should happen that a girl is too promiscuous to be able to settle down in marriage, her father, not having received cattle for her, can claim her children for his lineage.

The most ingenious elaboration of this legal principle is applied to the Nuer sentiment that no man should die without leaving legitimate descendants to carry on his name. If this should happen, his kinsmen are duty-bound to collect cattle and to use them to marry a woman to the dead man. His brother or nephew would normally take on the responsibility of begetting children whose place in the lineage genealogy would be as the dead man's offspring.

Looking at a Nuer village, with the identical home-steads and cattle kraals, it would be impossible to disentangle the elaborate skein of relationships between living and dead. A roster of the living men would not give all the fathers of babies being born. Dead persons are legally active, so much so that a man might inherit the widows of one brother and marry a girl to the name of another, and then, having piously begotten many children to the name be forgotten sets a limit on the social dangers— to carry on his own name. Then of course the altruistic obligation to marry a woman for his ghost falls on some-one else—and so on.

The honoring of this obligation has another aspect. Individual Nuer have to be ready to defend their rights with force. They risk maiming or death when they start a fight. The confidence that kinsmen would not let your name be forgotten sets a limit on the social dangers— if one can separate the physical risks from social risks. Fear of what would happen to his family and his own good name would not stop a man from laying his life on the line: the family would be cared for, and his name avenged and perpetuated. The system of accounting has to provide the conditions for its own smooth working at any level—psychological, intellectual, and institutional.

The Nuer find their way through this web of legal fictions because of the simple rule that they can either
marry or claim cattle and kinship. This rule working in
every sexual confrontation makes it easy for Nuer to see
the tribe as a single genealogical system. It also means
that every possible sexual adventure is an occasion on
which the relationship system had to be reviewed and
its principles reaffirmed.

Thus did Evans-Pritchard show how problems about
accountability develop muscle in the human faculties of
reasoning. The joint effort of creating Nuer society also
produces a powerful machinery for turning social dilemmas into legalistic issues, solved by fictions. But important though this was, it was not quite the big discovery
that psychologists in Bartlett's day would have needed
to put them on another trail of inquiry. The main interest to them should have been Evans-Pritchard's analysis
of how consciousness itself is structured.

Two approaches to this problem may be mentioned:
one was according to the idea that the individual does his
own work of accountability, sifting information and organizing it upon a personal evolving scheme, his social
interests being his guide (this approximates to Bartlett's
assumptions); the other (Halbwachs's), within the
French sociological tradition, took more deliberate account of social pressures and of physical aids to support
the meanings. Neither approach invited one to think of
the blanks in memory as being social constructs nor did
either suggest that the gaps over which recall is impossible are more than a mere incidental result of the structuring of attention by social interests. Yet amnesic blanks
are a crucial part of the social structuring, one of the
conditions of its smooth working. However, in the 1920s
no one transferred to sociology Freud's insight that some
forgetfulness in the individual is a blessed help to sanity.
Evans-Pritchard achieved this parallel insight for the

working of the social system. By so doing he anticipated contemporary work, such as Michel Foucault's, on socially constructed oblivion. He also cut the theory of memory free from physical props.

As he saw it, the Nuer articulate their experience of past time and anchor its several parts into the articulated society on which they focus attention. Most Nuer tribes have a history of only ten or eleven generations. There is good reason to think they have been in existence as tribes in that location much longer. As the tribe is thought of by Nuer as a genealogical structure, the anthropologist was bound to ask why the succeeding generations of the dead do not cumulatively lengthen the genealogical tree.

The answer, in Evans-Pritchard's work, is the concept of structural distance. Every Nuer can place himself genealogically in the tribe for two kinds of purposes: for calculating political alignment and for calculating sex and cattle trade-offs. Political alignment is determined by considering the major territorial divisions of the tribe, and the skeletal spread through them of the dominant clan. A tribe does not contain more than five or six levels of segmentation—from the most inclusive to the smallest local community. At the edges of the tribe the force of law runs out. Within each of its major divisions redress for wrongs becomes progressively easier until the last level, the local community, which is like a close-knit kinship unit. The first four or five generations of the tribe's existence from its founder to the more recently dead are continually commemorated in all the political confrontations in which a person has to assess wrongs as redressable or not. Structural distance being an active political principle, there is no difficulty in understanding how Nuer manage to remember the major levels of segmentation.

The other context for reckoning genealogy is the taking of women in marriage and the claiming and paying of cattle. In this context the reckoning of descent starts from the opposite direction. Any adult can easily recall the relationships of his father's father's father; there will be people alive and around who can corroborate. A descendant of the father's father's father may turn up at a girl's marriage and claim a calf. It would be given to him as a sign that the limit of claims has been reached at the fourth generation. Relatives who claim relationship up to six or seven generations back would not be refused a gift, but cattle claims are recognized up to and not including the fifth generation. Anyone who knows that this is how he is related, also knows that sexual intercourse with the range of girls thus defined as kin would count as incestuous.

By using one system for reckoning forward from the beginning of time and another for reckoning backward from the present day, the Nuer limit their historical experience. An amnesic space in the middle of the genealogy swallows up the new generations as the dead great-great-grandfathers are succeeded by new great-grandfathers. Thanks to this structural fault in the method of reckoning, an empty hole was created. Its absorbent properties reduce the whole known past and allow it to be articulated. If every generation were to be included, the impossible task of remembering everything would strain the cognitive schema. Lapses of memory would be individual and fortuitous instead of social and regular. The public structuring of the consciousness of time allowed the Nuer to take full cognizance of a short historical depth. The tree under which mankind came into being was still standing in western Nuerland until a few years before the research began.

The most important sentence in which Evans-Pritchard summed up the Nuer consciousness of time is: "Beyond the annual cycle, time-reckoning is a conceptualization of the social structure, and the points for reference are a projection into the past of actual relationships between persons." He did not consider the material benchmarks of time's passing as vitally important for sustaining memory. The hooves treading out paths over the land, as cattle are driven from one homestead to another, are material aids to memory, no doubt, but they would never take it very far back. There are no written constitutions, no enduring monuments, no scenes of battle or palace ruins. The maximum historical depth is achieved by the exigencies of the Nuer social structure: "Time is not a continuum, but is a constant structural relationship between two points, the first and last persons in a line of agnatic descent."[7]

These statements expand easily into a testable general hypothesis and a program for relating historical consciousness to social structure. If the Nuer case, which Evans-Pritchard demonstrated, has wider implications, then other people too use their conceptualizing of the social structure to give points of reference for projection into the past of actual social relations. Immediately after World War II, younger anthropologists took up this challenge. Evans-Pritchard had not explained the steps by which the present is projected into the past, nor did he himself attempt the comparative studies that would test the general applicability of the idea. The first exercise was performed by intensive fieldwork among the Tiv of southeast Nigeria. A whole process of clipping, eliding, and openly adjusting genealogies so that history would accord with the current distribution of authority was described in a basic form that deserves not to be forgotten.[8]

[7] *The Nuer*, p. 108.
[8] J. A. Barnes, *Politics in a Changing Society;* L. Bohannon, "A Genealogical Charter"; I. G. Cunnison, *The Luapula Peoples of Northern Rhodesia;* R. F. Murphy, "Tuary Kinship."

However, when the rewriting of science textbooks was shown to be performing exactly the same function in Western society—of keeping memory of the past in alignment with the present state of scientific authority[9]—it seems probable that the Tiv demonstration was not known or profited from.

A major point needs to be made about this later fulfillment of Bartlett's program: contrary to his expectation the peoples whose time experience is posited as being structured by their social experience must be credited with an active role in the analysis. The clipping, elision, and merging of sections of history is not something that is happening to them; it is something they are doing. They are very conscious agents. The Tiv who engage in disputes about political seniority derive some of their bargaining power from the numbers they can muster in support and some from ancient genealogical right: at the end of the day, when settlement is reached, sheer numerical strength always wins over genealogy; consequently the genealogical charter has to be amended to fit the political reality that has been accepted. Their negotiating is from a short-term perspective. They do not have in mind the final resultant structure of their society. What they do with one set of purposes creates the unintended empty spaces or the thick clusters of fine discriminations that characterize their consciousness.

Beside the sophistication of this work, other generalizations about the experience of time seem childish indeed. The extreme methodological positivism, the search for objective bases for comparison, the trial and testing of data are recognizably in the tradition of the empirical sciences, as austere in what they do allow themselves to conclude as in that which is rejected as evidence.

[9] T. S. Kuhn, *The Structure of Scientific Revolutions*.

Well before the self-fulfilling prophecy became a tag word in sociology, these self-limiting, self-validating processes of collective cognition were being analyzed in the 1940s in greater intricacy than has since been achieved. Well before phenomenology's claim that sociological understanding must start from the negotiating activities of conscious, intelligent agents, Evans-Pritchard had seized the problem, developed a method, and shown what progress can be made.

viii

Now we come to Evans-Pritchard's book on *Nuer Religion*, the climax of the series that started with the promise that everyday knowledge should be compared with everyday knowledge, technology with technology, and theology with theology. At this point a shortcoming of the whole program appears. When it was a matter of interpreting everyday meanings it was useful and needful to remove artificial fences between primitive and modern thought. But when it comes to comparing theologies, the same boundaries may not be artificial. One explicit theology cannot be compared with another unless explicit theologizing is going on in both places. Evans-Pritchard started out with a wish to be led into alien worlds, to conduct his life by oracles if need be, to find meanings in the full context of actions. But in this final book he straitjackets Nuer ideas by his own preformed judgment of what a book on religion should include. Nuer reflections on God, sin, sacrifice, spirit, symbolism are collected together for a moving theological statement.

Try to imagine a Nuer sage writing about Nuer religion; imagine him doing so without knowledge of the Western tradition and without intending to make Nuer experience accessible to Westerners. One should suppose he would plan his treatise very differently, choosing his key areas of exposition unpredictably, leaving major matters untouched, expatiating upon unexpected knotty problems. But there is no reason why a Nuer, living the life of a Nuer, should ever set about writing that book. The categories that give such treatises their life are the polemics of heterodoxy and orthodoxy. Neither is present in Nuer culture. The need to confound one's critics by theoretical synthesis belongs to a particular historical tradition.

If a great Talmudic scholar were to submit Nuer culture to analysis, he would no doubt set it in a characteristic Talmudic perspective. If a learned Buddhist had thought of scrutinizing Nuer religious behavior, he would fasten upon different elements. Presented by a Toltec priest or a Siberian shaman, each profound picture of Nuer religion would have been different. But the best interpretations would only fail to resemble the original in the minor ways that the Chinese drawing entitled "Cows in Derwentwater" does not immediately recall the English Lake District. Knobbly cows and trees stand in a Chinese style of landscape, but they are recognizably cows and trees, the lake, the misty mountain ridges are all there, checkable points of reference.[1]

Some writers belittle anthropological interpretation, maintaining that each effort betrays more of the contours

[1] Wash and ink (1936) in E. H. Gombrich, *Art and Illusion,* p. 86.

of the translator's mind than of the original. I would argue that to dismiss attempts at translation because they do not correspond to an imaginary native text is a peculiar manifestation of Western thought. Eventually that Western desire for an impossible objectivity must lead the philosopher to the blank edges of awareness. His pessimism about translation rests on a belief that he can never learn new things, only incorporate other people's experience within his usual categories. So he imagines interpretation as demanding an impossible leap from his own into another universe of thought. A more modest program is feasible if an attempt to interpret is seen as an inquiry within a conversation. The inquiry brings answers with it that change the next questions that can be asked. The inquirer's universe of knowledge itself is expandable. Evans-Pritchard adopted the task of explaining something important to his own generation. He determined that the proper method was comparative. For comparison between cultures, interpretation had to be tried. If he could alter the categories of his own generation's universe so that primitive peoples would rank in it as fully rational beings, that change would entail others, among them a higher status for religious knowledge in sociological thinking. His program was to translate by selecting the key words and dominant themes or motifs. (Stated baldly, as he frequently stated it, there is nothing in that program which guarantees that there will be checkable reference points from culture to culture.) He also insisted that crises of misfortune were the moments in which people revealed their central preoccupations so that the dominant themes could be recognized. To this rudimentary statement of his methodology I add that his actual analysis (as distinct from what he said he was doing) suggests a sound basis for translating and comparing cultures. In misfortune, people find ways of fixing accountability. Systems of accountability can be compared without departing from our steady foothold in our own scheme of knowledge, for they have checkable points of reference.

To treat alien theology as theology, Evans-Pritchard had to take theological scholarship seriously. He refreshed his knowledge of Greek philosophy, returned to the divinity books of his parsonage home, reread the Bible, consulted Hebrew scholars, and generally ransacked the resources of his own culture to the best of his ability. It is as if no design would be grand enough unless it set Nuer thought accurately in the framework of Plato's vast polarities, illuminated with the sharp distinctions of the Desert fathers.

To give an idea of how wholeheartedly Evans-Pritchard entered upon the exegesis of Nuer religion, confident that it must yield its meaning to full and sensitive inquiry, I will introduce the themes of divine love, ritual efficacy, and sin. The first, the assertion that the God of the Nuer can love, bore upon the contrary conviction, held by many missionaries, that primitive religion is based upon the emotion of fear. The second bore upon the widespread view that primitives performed magic instead of praying, expecting the rite to achieve results automatically. The third, the Nuer sense of merited punishment and their catalogue of sins, introduces the moral principles that explain the working of the feud and the automatic damper on political strife.

The book *Nuer Religion* starts with the conception of God. Immediately the flood of references to Hebrew and Greek ideas begins:

The Nuer *kwoth*, like the Latin *spiritus*, the Greek *pneuma*, and the English derivatives of both words, suggests both the intangible quality of air and the breathing or blowing out of air. Like the Hebrew *ruah* it is an onomatope and denotes violent breathing out of air in contrast to ordinary breathing. In its verbal form it is used to describe such actions as blowing on the embers of a fire; blowing on food to cool it; blowing into the uterus of a cow, while a tulchan is propped up before it, to make it give milk; snorting; the blowing out of air by the puff fish; and the hooting by steam pressure of a river steamer. The word is also found, and has the same general sense, in some of the other Nilotic languages.

As a noun, however, *kwoth* means only Spirit, and in the particular sense we are now discussing it means *kwoth nhial* or *kwoth a nhial,* Spirit of the heavens or Spirit who is in the heavens. . . .

It would equally be a mistake to regard the association of God with the sky as pure metaphor, for though the sky is not God, and though God is everywhere, he is thought of as being particularly in the sky. . . .[2]

In this first chapter, Evans-Pritchard sets out to show that the Nuer God is neither a thing of wood or stone nor anthropomorphic, but a spiritual conception. God is in the sky, he is not the same as the sky, he is everywhere, he is especially in the sky as men are especially on the earth. He has no real physical location, no spatial boundaries. Thus the first big dichotomy is drawn between the things of above, associated with spirit, and the things of below, associated with men. But the divide is bridged: God intervenes in men's affairs; his lightning may strike and kill a person whose spirit then is known as a child of God. Similarly, since divine intervention causes the birth of twins, twins are known as children of God and associated with high-flying and migratory birds.

The first pages of Evans-Pritchard's exposition lay out the grounds for anticipating later chapters on spirits of the below, spirits of the sky, soul and ghost.

The Nuer extend their genealogical concepts to the

physical universe and classify flora and fauna according to ascribed lineage relationships; it is not surprising that their conception of man's relations to God is in the model of human social relations. He is the father of men, he created them. Then the translation of the word to create has to be justified:

> God, Spirit in the heavens who is like wind and air, is the creator and mover of all things. Since he made the world he is addressed in prayers as *kwoth ghaua,* Spirit of the universe, with the sense of creator of the universe. The word *cak,* used as a noun, can mean the creation, that is, all created things. . . . As a verb "to create" it signifies creation *ex nihilo,* and when speaking of things can therefore only be used of God. However, the word can be used of men for imaginative constructions, such as the thinking of a name to give a child, inventing a tale, or composing a poem, in the same figurative sense as when we say that an actor creates a part. The word therefore means not only creation from nothing but also creation by thought or imagination, so that "God created the universe" has the sense of "God thought of the universe" or "God imagined the universe."[3]

Adding this together with much more, the Nuer God is presented as creative spirit, a living person; he is ubiquitous and invisible, he sees and hears all that happens, and he can be angry and can love.

Here follows the deft aside: "(the Nuer word is *nhok,* and if we translate it 'to love' it must be understood in the preferential sense of *agapo* or *diligo:* when Nuer say that God loves something, they mean he is partial to it)."[4] But how does the anthropologist know that they mean *agapo* by a word that could be translated love? As in the case of the word create, the choice of *agapo* turns out to

[3] Ibid., pp. 4–5.
[4] Ibid., p. 7.

be very deliberate. Instead of only one chapter, half the entire book expounds the relationship between the individual Nuer and the Nuer God. Evidently love of a theologically recognizable kind dominates the relationship. It is not difficult to describe it, following Evans-Pritchard's method of collecting Nuer spoken prayers, their spontaneous references, their solemn invocations at final sacrifices; above all their attitude to misfortune, their trust and childlike confidence. Readers should place the reference to *agapo* in the context of all the possible relations between gods and their devotees. There are many religions known to history in which gods desiring the sexual love of humans, charm, seduce, rape, or otherwise take physical possession of them. There are religions also in which humans seek passionately for union with their gods and even achieve divinity for themselves. Fasting, vigils, feats of endurance, and trance-inducing techniques compel the deity to reciprocate their longing.

The Lutheran theologian Anders Nygren recommended a method of comparing religions by what he called their fundamental motifs. Evans-Pritchard acknowledges Nygren[5] and was influenced by him. It is worth placing side by side their remarks about method. Nygren traced the development of Christianity as a conflict between two concepts of love, the Hellenistic concept of *eros* and the novel Christian concept of *agape, eros* being the Platonic idea of motivated love, *agape* being self-giving, disinterested love given by God to his creatures. Justifying his focus on these themes, he said:

> There is quite concrete proof of the existence both of another attitude to life of which the hallmark is *Eros*, and equally concrete proof of the existence of another attitude to life of which the hallmark is *Agape*, and

[5] *Essays in Social Anthropology*, p. 54; *Theories of Primitive Religion*, p. 14.

these two general attitudes do not run side by side like parallel lines that never meet, but they constantly run into one another. At any point in the history of the spiritual life there is concrete evidence of a relation between them, inasmuch as each strives to put its stamp on the spiritual life as a whole. When we speak of *Eros* and *Agape*, therefore, we are thinking of them all the time in this sense—that is, as "fundamental motifs." . . . The term "fundamental motif" requires more precise definition. . . . The most important task of those engaged in the more scientific study of religion and theological research is to reach an inner understanding of the different forms of religion in the light of their different fundamental motifs. For a long time they have been chiefly occupied in collecting a vast mass of material drawn from different religious sources for the purposes of comparison. But when the comparison actually comes to be made, the uncertainty of it immediately becomes apparent; for it is plain that no conclusion can be drawn from the mere fact that one and the same idea occurs in different religious contexts. The idea of belief may have exactly the same form without having at all the same meaning, if in one case it is a basic conception, while in another it is more loosely attached. . . . In other words we must try to see what is the basic idea or the driving power of the religion concerned, or what it is that gives it its character as a whole and communicates to all parts its special content and color. It is the attempt to carry out such a structural analysis, whether in the matter of religion or elsewhere, that we describe as motif research.[6]

At the end of *Nuer Religion*, Evans-Pritchard wrote:

We have, therefore, in the study of primitive philosophies to begin anew to build up a theory and to formulate problems in the light of it. There is only one way in which this can be done. A number of systematic studies or primitive philosophies has to be made. When

[6] A. Nygren, *Agape and Eros*, p. 35.

that has been done a classification can be made on the basis of which comparative studies can be undertaken which possibly may lead to some general conclusions. . . .

Such a classification of African philosophies must naturally be by reference to their chief and characteristic features. Among all African peoples we find in one form or another theistic beliefs, manistic cults, witchcraft notions, interdictions with supernatural sanctions, magical practices, &c., but the philosophy of each has its own special character in virtue of the way in which among that people these ideas are related to one another. It will be found that one or other belief, or set of beliefs, dominates the others and gives form, pattern, and color to the whole. Thus, among some peoples, notably a large proportion of the Bantu, the dominant motif is provided by the cult of ancestors; among others, some of the Sudanic peoples for example, it is found in the notion of witchcraft, with which are bound up magical and oracular techniques; among others, such as the Nuer, Spirit is in the centre of the picture and manistic and witchcraft ideas are peripheral; and among other peoples yet other notions predominate. The test of what is the dominant motif is usually, perhaps always, to what a people attribute dangers and sickness and other misfortunes and what steps they take to avoid or eliminate them.[7]

According to Nygren the first four centuries of Christian history had witnessed a new fundamental motif of religion and ethics, the *agape* motif. It struggled with the *nomos*, or legalistic motif of Judaism, and the spiritualizing, divinizing motif of *eros* in Greek religion, which allowed man to reach up to God and even aspire to divinity. The religions prior to Christianity extended to humans the possibility of deserving or attracting God's love, meriting it. The original Christian *agape* motif found all the initiative with God, rejecting the pride of man and the

[7] *Nuer Religion*, p. 315.

diminishing of godhead implied by any doctrine of man's ability to reach upward. But by the end of the fourth century the *agape* motif was not dominant. Then Augustine developed a new synthesis, the *caritas* motif. This vigorous hybrid of love from God and love to God, according to Nygren, by dominating Catholic medieval theology allowed anthropocentric theories of merit and vainglorious works to creep back into a religion from which they had originally been rejected.

Under anthropocentric Nygren grouped all the religious motifs before and after *agape,* teaching that this distinctive theocentric motif was often threatened in the history of Christianity and even submerged. Luther "discovered the *eros* feature of the *caritas*-synthesis. He therefore had to destroy it to make room for Christian love."[8]

Nygren only used the contrast between anthropocentric and theocentric religions to clarify his reading of Christian church history. He did not pretend to offer any exhaustive typology for comparative religion. He wrote as the committed Lutheran expositor, the future president of the World Lutheran Foundation. Yet this simple typology is very rich and suggestive for comparative religion. Any doctrinal scope for laying love obligations on God implies fundamental adaptations in the rest of religious doctrine: God could have favorites; the unfavored would fare less well in arbitrary judgments and distributions; doctrines of retribution would be revised away from universal categories; God's judgment might be misted by passion; the concept of law would be weaker; the whole universe would be seen differently. Especially would the response to misfortune be radically different, compared with a religion dominated by *agape.*

Evans-Pritchard did not try to make typologies, declaring the state of knowledge to be inadequate. When he

[8] A. Nygren, *Agape and Eros,* p. 72.

says that the Nuer attribute a selfless love to God, Nygren's interpretative framework is explicit.[9] Then for sure it becomes obvious, through everything the Nuer say and do about their wishes and misfortunes in daily life, that theirs is a theocentric religion and that *agape* is the closest word for *nhok*, when *nhok* is applied to God.

When there is a crisis and they do not know what to do, the Nuer comfort themselves saying God is present with them and will help them.[10] A ne'er-do-well asked how he expected to live might reply: God is limitless (in his power to aid).[11] The recital of their intimate, informal prayers and their resignation in the face of adversity build up the theme that they do not expect to sway him. God is always in the right, the founder and guardian of morality. Up to a point the Nuer can avert trouble by behaving well. When the anthropologist was ill, they would come and say gently:

"Well, pray to God and tell him that you have come on a journey to the country of the Nuer and that you have not hit anyone or stolen anything or done any bad thing there, and then he will leave you alone"; or "It is nothing. You will not die. This is our earth and you shall not die on it. Why should you die? You have not wronged us, and you are friend to all our children." . . . As these admonitions imply, if a man does wrong God will sooner or later punish him.[12]

But wrongdoing is not the only explanation for affliction. God can do what he likes with his own.

Nuer accept misfortunes with resignation. Whatever the occasion of death and other misfortunes may be, whether they be what Nuer call *dung cak,* the lot of

[9] *Theories of Primitive Religion,* p. 14; *Essays in Social Anthropology,* p. 54; *Nuer Religion,* p. 317.
[10] *Nuer Religion,* p. 9.
[11] Ibid., p. 4.
[12] Ibid., p. 17.

created things, or whether they be the result of what
they call *dueri*, faults, they come to one and all alike,
and Nuer say that they must be accepted as the will of
God. . . . When a child dies women lament, but only
for a little while, and men are silent. They say that
God has taken his own and that they must not complain; perhaps he will give them another child. . . .
Likewise if a cow or an ox of your herd dies Nuer say
that you must not complain if God takes his own beast.
The cattle of your herd are his and not yours. If you
grieve overmuch God will be angry that you resent his
taking what is his. Better be content, therefore, that
God should do what he wishes, seeing not that he has
taken one of your cows but that he has spared the
others. If you forget the cow God will see that you are
poor and will spare you and your children and your
other beasts. I cannot convey the Nuer attitude better
than by quoting the Book of Job: "the Lord gave, and
the Lord hath taken away; blessed be the name of the
Lord" (I. 21).[13]

Many more passages show the Nuer admitting their
feebleness, smallness, stupidity before God. This is in
striking contrast to their overbearing pride before any
other humans. Before God they are like ants, so small,
like idiots, so simpleminded.

Nygren showed great insight when he clustered together characteristic Lutheran Christian forms at one
pole of the historical comparison, calling them theocentric, in contrast with anthropocentric religions. Sure
enough, the Nuer sense of the chasm between godhead
and created things entails several other ideas that link
to make the predicted pattern. Nuer passivity in the face
of misfortune that they could not attribute to human responsibility was complementary to their pugnacity in all
other cases. Their resignation when God was seen to have
intervened was as brave as their resistance to damage

[13] Ibid., p. 12.

caused by another person. The two kinds of accountability supported each other by their grounding in the concept of "being in the right." A man knew when he was in the right in any human transaction because kinsmen showed that they agreed, by fighting with him. Their mutual liabilities being precisely detailed and put to the test, uncertainty was reduced. But this was not possible in relation with God, for God always had the right on his side. Being in the right was a much more central idea to this cosmology than loving. Yet, as its implications unfold, Nygren's predicted correlatives of a religion based on a particular doctrine of love and responsibility emerge. If Evans-Pritchard wanted to interpret an exotic religion in a way that would be intelligible within the Judeo-Christian tradition, he could hardly do better than present Nygren's thesis.

One bias in Nuer behavior is especially significant for comparison with Christian doctrinal history: their emphasis on intention in the justification of man before God. Right intention as distinct from right ritual focused the bitterest controversies of the Reformation and remains the most frequently used of Christian religious typologies. On the one hand, a trend to formalism, the preference for prescribed performance of ritual, on the other a preference for spontaneity, sincerity, directness: formalism places value on public worship, spontaneity prefers private worship. The advocates of spontaneity will tend to treat intention as the only effective means of attracting God's aid, while the advocates of formalism will tend to prescribe efficacious rites. When efficacy can be attributed to actions and things, the way is open for commerce in them. One point of view entails another and another until the initial contrast takes us all the way back to Luther's attack on clerical corruption, simony, and the sale of indulgences. It also embraces the difference between prayer and magic; reformation apologetics associated Protestantism with prayer and Catholicism with magic so explicitly that five centuries later W. Robertson Smith could draw up a plausible scale of moral evolution showing Catholicism and other magic-ridden religions being outdistanced by more ethical, spiritual forms of belief.[14]

Taking God to be the guardian of the moral order, the Nuer believe him to be more concerned with intention than with action, as are they themselves in their dealings with one another. They pay less compensation for killing a man by a fishing spear or a club than with a fighting spear, for it was less likely to be premeditated:[15]

> When I was living on the Sobat river news came to our village that some persons in an upstream village had found some meat and had cooked and eaten it, thinking that it was the flesh of some animal crocodiles had mutilated, and that they had later discovered it to be the flesh of a man whom crocodiles had killed and torn to pieces. I was told that these persons would at once have taken *wal nueera*, medicine to cleanse them from pollution, and that while the happening was very disgusting it was unlikely that it would cause death because the flesh was eaten in ignorance of its nature. Nuer say that God may overlook what was done in error. Similarly, they say that he will not allow a curse to harm a man who has done no deliberate wrong.[16]

There is still a sense in which a wrong act is always a wrong act, whether deliberate or not. In their accounting with each other, the Nuer have a fair chance of winning because they all know the rules. But in their accounting with God, the ambiguities and possible consequences overwhelm the case they might like to make. Between

[14] *The Religion of the Semites.*
[15] *Nuer Religion*, p. 107.
[16] Ibid., pp. 17–18.

man and God, man cannot win, even by the most scrupulous observance of the moral law, for human faults are
inevitable and accumulate. In the end God's adverse
judgment will catch up with them. The same for sacrifice, the high moment in man's relation with God: it is
not a magical act designed to produce prosperity. Three
chapters in Evans-Pritchard's book explain it as the
central framework of their relation to God, expressing
everything they know, their identification with cattle,
with kin, their knowledge of sin, their trust and faith.
On all the important points, the Nuer would be aligned
with Protestants and advanced religion. This should have
come as a great surprise to professors of comparative religion, and if he had known about it, would have been a
real problem for Nygren's thesis that the *agape* motif was
unique to Christianity.

Since I do not intend to follow his entire book through
its analysis of soul, ghost, totems, and spear symbolism,
I may diverge from its path to mention that sacrificing
cattle is one of the ways that the Nuer put pressure on
each other and recognize claims. If one pays attention
through the book to Nuer occasions of sacrifice, one rec-
ognizes trails cut by relations traveling from far to attend
this funeral or that purification or peacemaking. In this
way kinship claims are made evident at sacrificial rites,
by the ostentatious effort of traipsing across the country
to be there. Religion provides another medium in which
people confront one another and require that deeds support sentiments. Presence at sacrifices constitutes kinship
and is part of the legitimizing background for claims to
cattle or wives. Religion, then, is a double set of accounts:
it enables people to hold each other accountable to a
common commitment to rituals which testify to their
right-mindedness; it also provides a balance sheet on
which their relation to God can be assessed.

It is true the Nuer do not take a formalistic magical approach to get the prosperity they desire, but when it comes to reckoning the causes of disaster, they are very precise and formal. Each class of sin is tallied against a class of illness which it will cause. Enteritis is a sign of one kind of offense, eczema another, backache another. No matter what the cause, the cure is always a sacrifice. And here the casuistic grading of big and little offenses adjusts the gravity of sins to the value of the beast to be offered. God, being just and all-knowing, will even accept a wild cucumber in token sacrifice for an ox promised for later. But the spirits are greedy and less considerate. A man may be forced to drive hard bargains with them. The owner of a herd of cattle has to meet several different kinds of claims against them, first the claim of his dependents to have milk to drink, second the demand to kill livestock to pay heavenly debts, and third, the demand to let them be driven away in payment of social debts.

If a man were to refuse to pay up in the social transactions, the whole system would collapse like a pack of cards. It is no small political achievement that any Nuer to whom a cow is owing can go and collect his debt in a camp of strangers with all the immunities of law. The pressure of cattle debts being strong, the wish to evade payment must be strong also. The possibility of fighting it out when one has had the misfortune to kill another must be more attractive than paying over full forty head of cattle. However, the social debts tend to get paid, within geographical and social limits. As we have seen, these payments create communities which recognize their own distinct identity and that are able to ally with neighbors to defend their rights against more distant foes. But the regular fission and fusion that brings strife to a truce when balanced segments confront each other depend on the imbalance in transactions between God and man.

God's being heavily in the right allows the Nuer to set a limit to claims. Radiating out from anyone's homestead, there are borderline conflicts where the limit to claims has been reached. Men may not lay all their sorrows to the door of fellow men. God is responsible for the most grievous. Or rather, they accept that their disasters are God's penalties on them for acts for which they are responsible. There is a limit to claiming and blaming. The friends of an afflicted man press him to accept his troubles as coming from God. No one can claim redress for hidden psychic sources of damage; no searching of oracles to know who is bewitching sick children or casting a murrain on the cow. Accepting God's judicial interventions, accepting themselves as always in the wrong in his sight, means a limit to claims.

Further, all the rules of a self-equilibrating system of vengeance and self-help work homeostatically because God makes rightful claims. Making themselves responsible to God, they make God ultimately responsible. In many political systems based on self-help, vendetta killing escalates indefinitely. The Nuer can force each other to settle their feuds with fixed transfers of cattle, because human affairs are never capable of balancing out with God. Like playing a game in which the dealer is always bound to win: the stakes may as well be lowered because no one is going to win against God. The heavy debt in the divine accountability enables the other set of accounts to balance out. The rates at which human accountability is reckoned can be settled arbitrarily by conventions unquestioningly applied. The accumulated debt to God is a kind of cushion that absorbs the unaccountable shocks from social life. God takes a long time to make good his claims, but in the end, his justice catches up with the most secret defaulter. Since God is on the side of right, he is the collector of debts for those who cannot do so for themselves, and the thought of his heavy-handed intervention encourages payment. It is as if his eye for detail were extremely sharp; he even notes the origin of cattle in a homestead: if a woman for whose marriage they have been paid, or a wronged husband to whom they came in compensation for adultery, were to drink milk of the cows, sickness will befall. God does not cause it directly, but has set up the retributive universe. By requiring respect for cows given for different particular purposes, God's universe requires the Nuer to respect those purposes. He even punishes a man who fails to respect his in-laws by appearing improperly dressed in their presence. Collecting dues in the form of sickness and expiatory sacrifice for neglecting these intimate forms of respect, God upholds the moral law where no human has a private claim. He causes mortal sickness for a whole community when homicide among its members makes it likely that the kin of the slayer and kin of the victim drink the same water. Here he is collecting a claim that no one in the community can collect, because the feud would normally divide it into two internecine camps. When he punishes an incestuous couple, he upholds the principle by which everyone else regulates their accounts, namely that "where the women are, the cattle are not," based on the rule that one person cannot both give cattle and receive cattle in the same situation. When he punishes adultery by afflicting an injured husband with backache, he might seem to be acting arbitrarily: the innocent party, not the guilty pair, bears the penalty. But no: the universe is not siding with lovers. Whether the husband knows or does not know about the adultery, his backache makes him a victim of his wife's seducer— if he were to die the adulterer will be forced by the rest of the community to pay the full blood-compensation for taking a life. This belief is as good a way as any that has been devised for flushing out the secret adulterer, forcing him to confess and pay for the sacrifice lest the husband's illness worsen and a suit for adultery turn into a suit for homicide.

So one way or another each of the peculiar beliefs in the causes of illness fit together like a key in a lock. There is nothing unusual in itself in finding that God is collecting uncollectible claims on behalf of the wider community, or helping disadvantaged persons, wives, in-laws, and cuckolds to collect on their own behalf. Recalling the neurological model I mentioned in Chapter i, the Nuer God's righteousness irresistibly suggests Sherrington's distance perceptor—a delayed and sustained attention, stabilizing the organism as a whole. Evans-Pritchard had no trouble in resisting the mechanistic analogy. Yet I am sure that I have not oversystematized his thinking here. His style in *Nuer Religion*, while leisurely in quoting Nuer remarks, is terse in commentary upon them. The system appears in the way he constructed the trilogy. The first two books are especially condensed. To make the tight construction easier I have had to labor clumsily at pointing out connections between them and the third.

By the time that Evans-Pritchard finished his book on Nuer religion his initial program was complete. He had worked through the exercises required to establish a distinctive anthropological theory of knowledge. He could demonstrate the reasonableness of what seemed to be the wild flights of fancy, unbridled fears, haphazard mental associations, and mystic participations that were supposed to govern primitive thought. He first dismantled the imaginary constructs of earlier thinkers. He had to extract each piece of primitive theorizing, clean it, and get it into working order, then set it carefully back into its functioning context. He had to restore to their institutional setting thoughts that only seemed like nonsense because they had been abstracted and put into a false context. His own objective was clear and limited. He would not have dreamed of devaluing scientific knowledge. His frequent references to reality and objectivity made it clear that he accepted the views current in his own society about the nature of the world as it is. These views were neither his target nor something he was trying to defend. His readership would certainly have taken him for a lunatic if he adopted a relativist view, negating the possibility of comparing the values of kinds of knowledge. His target was within epistemology, and not concerned with the science of being. Consequently he assumed, from his declared standpoint, that the Azande were wrong about witchcraft and the Europeans were right. He would have lacked credibility if he had asked his colleagues to credit the Azande theory that a witch can leave his body sleeping in his bed and fly to a midnight necrophagous rendezvous, or any other such ideas from the history of witchcraft. To have raised the mere possibility that these ideas provided explanations of illness as sound as those found in our current state of medical knowledge would have roused the same intelligent opposition then as it would today. His strictures against earlier writers for their gross misunderstanding of primitive religions may have seemed to imply that they would have done better if they had been believers themselves instead of agnostics or atheists. But he is against that view. The anthropologist does not have to have a religion of his own.[17] The only mistake would be to carry forward into his interpretation of foreign beliefs any strong hostility or deep disagreement with religious believers from his own culture. Not being a theologian he is not concerned with the truth of religious ideas. A negative theological view, imported at the outset, to the

[17] *Theories of Primitive Religion,* p. 17.

effect that their religion is false, would be as damaging
to the anthropological inquiry as a negative judgment
passed prematurely on the value of their agricultural
techniques or an unqualified positive evaluation of their
medicine.

Primitive mentality had created a problem in psychology because the primitive was clearly wrong about
witches, ghosts, and zombies, and consistently wrong in
very interesting ways. Evans-Pritchard's answer was to
change the direction of inquiry away from objective
rightness and wrongness, and away from psychology
toward sociology and the workability of a system of ideas.
He tried to focus the discussion upon the service that
theories afford for ordinary life. His approach was the
consequence of a theoretical position stemming from the
assumptions of the French sociologists who had first
posed the problems in this form. They lacked empirical
procedures. He proposed to test and develop their ideas
by methodically tracking each verbal statement to its
context of action and, ultimately, to its place in a coherent system of accountability.

Evans-Pritchard's method provides nonarbitrary criteria for considering meaning. When he taught that
anthropology was more akin to history than to science,[18]
he was not denying the need for objectivity or the need
for classification and systematic comparison. He was
asking that field-workers be equipped with the insights
of the historian's discipline. A good example of the scientistic theorizing that he repudiated, and which is still in
disrepute, comes from Professor C. G. Seligman's Fore-
word to *Witchcraft, Oracles, and Magic among the
Azande*. It is generous, witty, and urbane. But at one or
two points we get a glimpse of what the book might have

[18] *Social Anthropology* (The Broadcast Lectures), p. 60; "Social Anthropology: Past and Present."

been like in other hands: "The Zande, as it seems, retains his infantile aggressive instincts through life, but unlike so many savages, he does not project these on to a more or less well-defined high God or on to the spirits of his ancestors."[19] Seligman also mentions introversion, normally associated with religion; extraversion, in this case associated with magic, animism, and he says that "something perhaps comparable to the 'censor" of Freud has come into existence and inhibited what we should call the common sense of the belief." At least Seligman credited the belief with common sense, but by other writers it could easily have been endowed with more anthropomorphic features and be set to play within some mechanical theory to attack, counteract, neutralize, or inhibit other beliefs.

By avoiding such conceits, beloved in the 1930s or 1940s, Evans-Pritchard stands clear of current criticisms of psychological theorizing. Consider a modern effort to disengage the insights of psychoanalysis from the distortions of functional analysis based on biological models. Roy Schafer argues that intentionality and personal meaning, the constituents of psychic reality and therefore the essential matter of psychoanalysis, are arbitrarily thinned and narrowed, reduced, and even excluded by the technical language of functions and energies; this is especially so for the concept of meaning.[20] Schafer's own preferred language for recasting the general theory so that it fits clinical practice is that of history. Evans-Pritchard called the trained historical imagination to his aid. In the same spirit, he was also inveighing against reductionist theories of religion. Sociological analysis was necessary, but wrong if it taught that the religious conceptions of primitive peoples were nothing more than symbolic

---

[19] *Witchcraft, Oracles, and Magic among the Azande*, p. xviii.
[20] R. Schafer, *A New Language for Psychoanalysis*, pp. 93–96.

representations of the social order.[21] What the person says the gods and spirits mean to him is as irreducible a datum as his statements about economic choice. The collective expression of religion has to be distinguished from the personal; from the first we learn more about the social order, from the second we learn what religion is. The Nuer conception of God cannot be reduced to or explained by the social order. When all the purely social and cultural forms have been abstracted, what is left is a description of a relationship between man and God. It transcends all forms, so not surprisingly the Nuer cannot tell us what is the nature of this spiritual relationship.[22]

Nothing can take us beyond the verbal metaphors, on the one hand, and the pledges of conviction, on the other. We can understand the metaphors insofar as we have a common experience over which translation is possible. But meanings will never yield to functional analysis. This is said to demarcate the limits of confidence for the anthropological quest for understanding. For Evans-Pritchard, the anthropologist's task is to trace meanings but not to pronounce them right or wrong.

[21] *Nuer Religion*, p. 313.
[22] *Nuer Religion*, p. 321.

Contradiction

ix

Anyone reading the preceding chapter may be struck by a contradiction: Evans-Pritchard's concern was to lower the artificial partitions between kinds of thought, especially primitive and modern; at the same time he recognized a difference between philosophizing and everyday thought. Here, evidently, are partitions he thought useful. In order to do justice to the philosophical depths of Nuer religious thought he had to dig up terms from old Christian controversies and contrast *agape* with *eros* in the senses used by Nygren. But the sharp-eyed critic will recall that the theologian had based his typology of religions on one kind of legalism, *nomos*, and three kinds of love, *agape*, *eros*, and *caritas*. Evans-Pritchard never mentioned the possibility of the Nuer religion being based on *caritas* or on *nomos*. But why not? Evidently the parallels he discerned between Lu-

theran and Nuer conceptions of grace and godhead were
so striking that it was enough of an argument to state
them.[1] If the critic conceded that major point, there are
still other difficulties in his text, not to be summarily
dismissed. Surely it goes against his own principles to
take the words of another civilization and use them to
make distinctions or to cover up contradictions that are
not observed in the culture being interpreted. Here we
are deep into anthropology's most difficult problems about
translation, and close to those original questions about
the thought processes of Indians who declare that they
are birds and apparently accept such a simple self-contradiction as true.

Evans-Pritchard dealt with apparent contradictions in
different ways. The Nuer statement that human twins are
birds he treated as an example of analogical thinking.
Because they are in the same class as birds, when Nuer
twins die they are not buried but their corpses are laid
across the forks of trees. Evans-Pritchard explained the
classification by depicting the general structure of Nuer
analogies by which God is to men as the sky above is to
the earth below, as birds are to land animals. The migratory birds that fly up and away, without being seen to
land, are especially like spirits, close to God. Humans
usually give birth to young singly; twin births are a sign
of divine intervention, so twins are to ordinary mortals
as birds are to animals, close to God, a manifestation of
spirit.

Among the Azande beliefs, he discovered some implicit
contradictions by tracing different lines of argument back
to statements that would be seen as contradictory if
Azande ever were to make them explicit, but which represented assumptions belonging to clearly segregated institutions which would never be brought into conflict in the

[1] *Nuer Religion*, pp. 317–18.

ordinary Azande experience. This corresponds to the bounding of curiosity as Bartlett described it. The incoherence detected in their thought is systematically related to the interlocking of their institutions.

A third way of dealing with apparent contradiction is to pursue the path of correct translation. It would be tempting to hope that with these three solutions—metaphor, separation of spheres of life, and good translation—all the apparent nonsenses of primitive thought could be interpreted as sense at one level or another. But the more conscientious the translation, the more a new problem about contradiction arises. It is probably wise for the ethnographer faced by paradox or contradiction to assume that by the end of the day, when he knows all the sentences held by the natives to be true, they will be found to make a coherent scheme. But the next example suggests that the assumption of ultimate coherence may be wrong.

Evans-Pritchard tried to decide whether Nuer religion was really monotheistic or polytheistic. When he saw a major contradiction, I believe he chose the wrong way to interpret it, importing a concept even more foreign and specialized than *agape* to bridge the gap.

It would be too simple to conclude, from the fact that they speak of gods in the plural, that the Nuer are polytheists. For one thing, Nuer insist that there is only one God.[2] But is the term god quite right for the idea? Evans-Pritchard could ask the question, "Do you believe in one god or in many?" but his rules of method forbade him to rely on their verbal answer to a verbal question. He had to observe that the singular and plural forms were used in different contexts. The question then turned on a difference of practice. When the Nuer use the singular form, the context refers to creator, father, judge, owner,

[2] Ibid., p. 48.

great spirit in heaven; while the plural form always refers to spirits of the air and to other spirits tied to particular places or lineages. God in the singular is the same great spirit for everyone, but these spirits in the plural have different importance for different people. Spirits in the plural may pass in and out of families, be remembered and forgotten, possess someone, make another sick, or otherwise make claims to respect. When a Nuer falls ill, if they cannot establish another cause, his relatives may get a prophet or diviner to examine the victim's family history or discover whether a forebear might not have had a spirit whom they have neglected.

After considering in detail all the contexts of sacrifice, consecration of cattle to spirits, and rite of exorcism, Evans-Pritchard tells us that there is no question of the Nuer regarding these spirits as beings of the same importance as God. "Whatever else they may be thought to be, they are not thought of as beings independent of and equal to him. There is only one God."[3] Among the facts he cited in evidence are the following linguistic usages. As they have no proper name for God, the Nuer cannot easily distinguish their God from the God of another people; though aware of their neighbors' differing religious beliefs, they regard them all as communicating with the same God as theirs, only under different titles. Apart from spirits attached to lineages and families, they also believe in spirits of the heavens. Any of these can be referred to individually, as a spirit but never as *the* spirit of heaven, that is, God. Referring to an individual spirit of heaven as relatively great compared with lesser ones, they can say: "a great spirit," never "the great spirit." The difference turns decisively on the use of the definite article. The Nuer call the spirits of the air children of God, to denote their lesser status below the Father-God

[3] Ibid., p. 48.

in the sky. They could be translated as godlings, angels, demons. The Nuer attitude to the spirits is as toward mischievous beings, exacting and jealous. God is above the capricious, greedy behavior they are credited with. The final test appears in the way the Nuer settle accounts with spirits: "in making amends through sacrifice a bargain is struck in a much cruder and more human way than when a sacrifice is made to God. The Nuer will bargain with a spirit, trying to buy it off as cheaply as he can, but never with God, and no Nuer would use such familiar terms in addressing God as he sometimes uses in addressing spirits."[4] The Nuer hold themselves accountable to God in a more serious way than their accountability to spirits. On these lines the case against their polytheism is sustained: there is one Nuer God and the other spirits are different and lesser.

At this point everything would be quite simple and straightforward, if only according to Nuer statements the spirits of the air were not also God; they are many and also one. The Nuer see no contradiction, so presumably their scrupulous ethnographer should not find a difficulty in passing as they do "from a more general and comprehensive way of conceiving God or Spirit to a more particular and limited way of conceiving God or Spirit, and back again. This is often very apparent in invocations made at their sacrifices and in what they say in times of sickness and other troubles. Therefore a question which tries to present a disjunction, an either . . . or, in answer to which either one proposition or the other may be accepted but not both, is not understood."[5] This problem is very different from the relation of analogy that holds between spirits and birds, twins and humans, so that twins are as birds. To translate the identity and differ-

[4] Ibid., p. 51.
[5] Ibid., pp. 51–52.

ence that affects the relation between the many spirits and the one God, Evans-Pritchard resorted to calling the spirits manifestations of God, local refractions of god-head.

The philosopher W. V. Quine has suggested that "wanton translation can make the natives sound as queer as one pleases. Better translation imposes our logic upon them."[6] He has also entered the caveat that the farther we get off home ground, the less sense there is in saying what is good translation or bad. Without a basis of comparison between two kinds of historical experience, there is little basis for translation. He gives as an example of this problem a little point of criticism made by Edmund Leach in elucidating some statements by Malinowski; Quine adds generously: "It is understandable that the further alternative of blaming the translation of conjunctions, copulas or other logical particles is nowhere considered; for any considerable complexity on the part of the English correlates of such words would of course present the working translator with forbidding practical difficulties."[7] It is worth recording that Evans-Pritchard was exceptional in not shirking these forbidding difficulties. As well as faithfully watching for the difference between a spirit and the spirit, Evans-Pritchard also scrupulously scouted out the verb to be, separating the senses of to exist, to be in the same class as, to be the same as. None of this helped him when the Nuer affirmed that the spirits were different from God and at the same time one with God. Spirits of the air, he said, "are not thought of as independent gods, but in some way as hypostases of the modes and attributes of a single God."[8] Hypostasis is a theological term meaning person of the

[6] W. V. Quine, *Word and Object*, p. 58.
[7] Ibid., p. 58; E. R. Leach, "The Epistemological Background to Malinowski's Empiricism," p. 130.
[8] *Nuer Religion*, pp. 49, 117.

godhead. If it were the correct term in this case, the spirits would not behave differently from God, capriciously or greedily, but as one person. We have the interesting case of a wrong term being introduced to resolve a contradiction that might worry us, did originally worry our own theologians, but that did not worry the Nuer. It was unnecessary to translate their thought by a term that had no equivalent in their language. The tolerance of one and many as noncontradictory or a mystery is common to many religions at different levels—Islam, Buddhism, and popular Christianity. In Christian cultic practice not only God but also the Virgin Mary is seen as one and many: as one historical person, efficacious in prayer, she is also manifest in numerous shrines and statues each having different material efficacies, godlike but more human than God and not above demanding special attention and exacting small revenges. The same meticulous labors of interpretation bestowed on the Spanish, Irish, and Italian Catholics would reveal their godlike pantheons of powerful archangels and saints. One upshot of the exercise is to make the words polytheism and monotheism not be lightly used. At best an immense labor of ethnography must go into determining their sense. Another upshot is to show the deformation of thought that is risked by the interpreter who is determined to make everything somehow translatable.

We feel a very different mood pervade Godfrey Lienhardt's book on Dinka thought. Lienhardt, a close friend and associate of Evans-Pritchard, went to study these neighbors of the Nuer. Seen from the Nuer viewpoint, the Dinka appeared in *Nuer Religion* as more magic-minded. When Evans-Pritchard reported mechanical approaches to God, divination, and fetishes among the Nuer, he always noted that they were said to be of recent origin, imported from the Dinka. The Nuer individual's habit of praying to God out loud when in trouble occasioned much surprise among the Dinka. One way and another *Nuer Religion* leads us to expect the Dinka religion to be more materialist, more fetishist than Nuer forms of spirituality.

Evans-Pritchard would have been disappointed if Lienhardt's Dinka study had slavishly followed the lines of his own, but no danger of that. Here is an anthropologist, profiting from the earlier work, avoiding its mistakes, and leaning over backward not to impose his own logic. Lienhardt starts by explaining why he prefers not to use the word God at all. Divinity with a capital D stands for the central concept of immanent creator, and divinity writ small for the lesser manifestations. He does not address the set of questions normally associated with theology. Every page of his book shows how inappropriate and misleading it would be to carve an old-fashioned, strictly theological topic out of the lives of people whose whole consciousness is informed by the experience of divinity. He broadens his focus to the fundamental questions in the psychology of perception: not merely how misfortune is perceived, as Evans-Pritchard taught, but even how space and color are perceived. Ultimately, I suppose, Lienhardt's book approaches the old question of how magic gets credence. But the method assumes a total suspension of belief, going beyond the credibility of magic to the point at which it can be asked how anything is credible, ever. Why does anyone ever consent to any version of reality? The answer comes in the many-tiered levels of sense that public rituals affirm. Liturgy endows action with meanings; the received meanings define perceptions and enclose interpretations.

This treatment does not need archaic medieval terminology to reveal the philosophical depth and subtlety of Dinka thought. By unpressured advance the analysis goes from interpreting very simple acts (the herdsman's knotting of a twist of grass to delay supper till his return) to violent sacrificial killings (the red ox that symbolizes the main divinity, Flesh) and emotive scenes of burial alive (the famous priest insisting on his right to be placed dying in his grave, his last breath to be kept in his body for a final benefit to his community). Perhaps the most extraordinary analysis is of this divinity, Flesh, and its hereditary priests. Whereas lesser divinities are manifested in different animal or other emblems, Flesh is the life in the living being. It is the divinity of cool judgment, clear light, truth, discernment. Its worshippers feel it stirring in their bodies, making them tremble and fall into ecstatic trance when invocations are chanted.

The divinity Flesh has as its emblems real flesh and blood, primarily in the bodies of men, the masters of the fishing-spear. There is a ceremony for "feeding" the Flesh in their bodies, though I have never seen it. It is said that at certain sacrifices to the divinity Flesh, which unlike other sacrifices take place at night, masters of the fishing-spear take small pieces of raw flesh from the victim and eat them with great solemnity before day breaks.* A master of the fishing-spear of the clan Paghol, which has the primacy in the Apuk Patuan tribe of the Rek, said that he would very respectfully take three small pieces of raw flesh from the thigh of an ox sacrificed for Flesh,† and would eat them to feed (augment) the Flesh. . . . They are ob-

* Cf. W. Robertson Smith, *Lectures on the Religion of the Semites*, note to p. 221 of the 1907 edition: ". . . certain Saracen sacrifices, nearly akin to the Passover, which were even eaten raw, and had to be entirely consumed before the sun rose. In this case the idea was that the efficacy of the sacrifice lay in the living flesh and blood of the victim. Everything of the nature of putrefaction was therefore to be avoided. . . ."
† Thigh and Thigh-bone is the principal divinity of this clan.[9]
[9] G. Lienhardt, *Divinity and Experience: The Religion of the Dinka*, pp. 143-44.

servances connected exclusively with masters of the fishing-spear, and they set them apart from others in sharing a mystery which others do not share. It is said that the "red" beasts sacrificed for the divinity Flesh are to be consumed utterly by the elders of their community in a byre at night, after the sacrifice. This is the only case of a solemn eating of the clan-divinity.

This passage illustrates the temptations resisted. Lienhardt relegated the Passover parallel to a footnote citing Robertson Smith; the Christian Eucharistic parallels are not mentioned at all. On the one hand, Lienhardt's field research does not seek to reveal an accountability system or base an articulated system of thought upon a system of social action. However, on the other hand, the Dinka ethnography is a better fulfillment of Evans-Pritchard's project than subsequent studies of religion, which were more reductionist and less attentive to philosophical insights. Earlier, I compared Evans-Pritchard's idea of understanding language always in its practical functions with Wittgenstein's comparison of language with an instruction manual. It would sadly miss the mark if this approach implied that language in action could not open out to embrace all human intentions and syntheses, if it could not make poetry as well as build ships.

One way to assess Evans-Pritchard's achievement is to see how many old questions have been laid to rest and new ones are now in play. The difference between a systematized dogmatic theology and the theological constructions of everyday life are now much clearer. The idea that there will be no contradictions in everyday thinking has been tried and rejected. Furthermore, contradictions at the level of everyday thinking are no longer a sign of intellectual weakness. Lienhardt's development from Evans-Pritchard's work leads us to expect insoluble antinomies to arise at deep levels of inquiry.

The ship-building manual would have to be consistent throughout, but one would expect metaphysical assumptions inevitably to involve contradiction if transferred to superficial levels of explanation. At more profound depths of understanding large incompatible assumptions about life and death and truth may be held together in unresolved conflict to fulfill the interpretive requirements of human society.

Evans-Pritchard's Contemporary Influence

The concluding chapter is the place to check
statements made earlier that may seem too sweep-
ing or tendentious. It has not been difficult to
place Evans-Pritchard in relation to his predecessors, they having earned their clearer outline by
the passage of time: compared with the poetic
speculations of Marett or Frazer, or with the rigid
scheme of Lévy-Bruhl, or with Bartlett's failure
to develop a sociological theory of perception, or
with Haddon's theory of conventionalizing, Evans-
Pritchard seems to speak to us with the lonely
voice of common sense. But if this story were
only to record the victory of plain thinking over
theorizing, it would be a dull tale and discourag-
ing to theorists. For common sense is prejudiced
and hasty in judgment; it is not likely to be always right, and it cannot take the place of theoretical method. However, when we try to compare

Evans-Pritchard with his own contemporaries, assessment of his work becomes more worthwhile—though much more difficult. We must start by separating off, as not strictly relevant, the work of those of his generation who had no special interest in the theory of knowledge or in any problems of human cognition. Though this seems arbitrarily to exclude a number of important contemporaries whose concern lay with political science or economics, Evans-Pritchard himself did some such bracketing off from his own concerns when he listed the large number of studies in anthropology that did not attempt to contribute directly to the understanding of thought systems.[1]

I should mention some apparently relevant movements in cultural analysis in the United States. From the beginning of this century two common ideas in philosophical commentary have found a sympathetic and quasi-technical niche in anthropology: one is the assumption of cultural holism, the other the separation of culture from behavior. The first gave rise to easy writing about world views, cultural patterns, central motifs, dominant themes, configurations of culture. The second allowed these cultural patterns to be considered as autonomous or at least as capable of being analyzed independently of social organization.[2]

None of the practitioners of cultural analysis developed a method for relating the levels of behavior which their initial assumptions had split apart, nor for overcoming the temptation to compose wholes out of a quick subjective intuition about how the elements of a culture seem to cohere. Writing about culture, Evans-Pritchard was concerned to find an objective method of justifying

---

[1] *Theories of Primitive Religion*, pp. 112–13.
[2] A good, short account of the problems of investigating culture in this sense of shared meanings cut off from shared economy and shared politics is given by Z. Bauman in *Culture as Praxis*.

his own interpretation. As I have reiterated, the method was to trace the discriminations that are made by people holding one another accountable. This includes steward-ship over material possessions and all other moral justi-fications. This method set a new standard for fieldwork which vaguer formulations of the problem did not re-quire, and provoked new specialized kinds of inquiry. So, though they seem relevant, the work of anthropolo-gists on the American side of the Atlantic in the 1930s and 1940s went in a different direction and addressed different problems.

The same can be said of a postwar generation of an-thropologists whose reaction against the looser style of their seniors in cultural anthropology created ethno-science and cognitive anthropology. These subspecialties are indeed sensitive to the problem of subjective bias and good translation. To meet the challenge of interpretation over exotic areas, they select a set of coordinates com-mon to each language, and use componential analysis to identify areas of overlapping or divergent meaning within a micro-scale domain.[3] But a convincing passage from this degree of accuracy to full-scale ethnography has never been demonstrated. The methods and inten-tions are so much closer to those of linguistics that it is safe to exclude these scientists from a record of those whose work is close to that of Evans-Pritchard.

Among British anthropologists it is difficult to separate the various strands of their interests. Many were close collaborators, interested in the same problems, and them-selves also all influenced by Radcliffe-Brown, Malinowski, and the French sociologists. For example, one of his closest colleagues is Meyer Fortes, whose original work on personal identity and on filial relations uses the same general principles of validation. It is a fully independent

[3] S. A. Tyler, "Introduction," in *Cognitive Anthropology*.

corpus, its roots in psychoanalytic theory, its materials from west Africa, its style of questioning and testing all its own. Yet the effect of having grown alongside the growth of Evans-Pritchard's work is undeniable. Comparisons of different kinds of blame-pinning that culminate in sorcery and witchcraft accusations proved a rich seam in African ethnography in the 1950s and later, taking the insights of the Azande study to more dynamic styles of political analysis.[4] A host of concerns that have radiated out from shared work include Horton's comparisons of local theories of personality and their accompanying variations in social experience, sociological perspectives on religious conversion, and on types of acceptable explanation. Comparative religious studies have been influenced by interpretations of spirit possession[5] and of ancestral cults,[6] analysis of the social and political differences likely to be found with variant forms of monotheism[7] and the everyday role of ritual in shaping cognized reality.[8] It is also important to record Evans-Pritchard's profound influence on a generation of Oxford historians.[9]

I should also mention Evans-Pritchard's encouragement to a new young field of Mediterranean anthropology[10] and his influence on Islamic studies.[11] At the same

[4] See the works of J. C. Mitchell, M. G. Marwick, I. Schapera, J. Middleton and E. H. Winter, M. Douglas, and V. W. Turner cited in the Short Bibliography.

[5] See the works of P. Fry, I. I. Zaretsky, and C. Shambaugh, J. Beattie and J. Middleton, E. Colson, and I. M. Lewis cited in the Short Bibliography.

[6] See J. Middleton, *Lugbara Religion* and T. O. Beidelman, "The Ox and Nuer Sacrifice."

[7] See B. C. Ray, *African Religions.*

[8] See J. Buxton, *Religion and Healing in Mandari,* and T. O. Beidelman, "Some Nuer Notions of Nakedness, Nudity, and Sexuality."

[9] See K. Thomas, "Should Historians Be Anthropologists?"

[10] See the works of J. G. Peristiany, J. Pitt-Rivers, and J. Davis cited in the Short Bibliography.

[11] See the works of E. L. Peters, E. Gellner, I. M. Lewis, A. P. Stirling, and S. M. Salim cited in the Short Bibliography.

time, he was encouraging Rodney Needham's translations of the French Thinkers of the Année Sociologique
group, and overseeing with Godfrey Lienhardt the scholarly publication by the Clarendon Press of African texts
side by side with English translations.

At this close focus upon such a large collaboration
it is impossible to give definition to the distinctive work
of scholars who were his friends and who influenced
him as well as he influenced them. Since a man is partly
to be judged by his friends, the confused attribution is a
part of the picture. In the era of postwar expansion,
British anthropologists had become much more profes-
sional than their immediate prewar predecessors and
more sociologically inclined in their outlook than American contemporaries. They shared ideas and argued vehe-
mently in that close atmosphere of competitive scholarship which is splendid for beating definitions into shape,
though less well adapted for spreading a message beyond
the ranks of the initiated.

After this overview of detailed interactions, it is necessary to paint with the big brush. In this past quarter-
century three outstanding names represent the world's
most famous work on human thinking processes: Piaget
on learning, Lévi-Strauss on culture, Noam Chomsky on
language. Their work represents three developments
from the ideas about primitive mentality of the early
decades of this century. Chomsky attends to the innate
capabilities of the human mind, Piaget to its developmental process. Both are interested in phylogenetic
questions—how the human faculties are organized and
what the limits to their capabilities may be; both implicitly expect their questions to lead back to the physiology
of the brain. Clearly the direction they follow is very
different from the researches just outlined. Much closer
is Lévi-Strauss's chosen path, for while he, too, is interested in the innate structure of the human mind, he

traces the relation between forms of rationality and social factors, and takes problems about primitive modes of
classification seriously. If I may indulge in the privilege
of posterity, I would simplify by saying that he illumi-
nates the paradoxes of totemism in two grand moves.
First, he puts an end to separate inquiries about itemized
peculiarities of totemic belief, requiring it rather to be
set out on the larger canvas of all analogic thinking
about classes of humans and classes of animals. Primitive thought, he argues, is dominated not by the means-
end chains of inference that leads to work but by a controlled exercise in metaphorical construction. He devel-
ops and popularizes a method of structural analysis that
makes sense of what once seemed nonsense, the sense of
analogy in place of the nonsense of contradiction. Although he works in the recalcitrant materials of ethnography, his method applies to any literary work of art. By
virtue of his own command of matter and style, he fuses
together what had, since Frazer's decline, become two
separate fields, civilized literature and primitive myth-
ology. Second, he neither began nor rested with a demonstration of the literary and philosophical power of
mythological imagery. Originally he developed a typology
of kinship and marriage and always sought to relate it to
totemic and other modes of thought. Against the dazzle
of his success, the contribution of his contemporaries
must seem pale. But what he has achieved takes us only
a certain way along the path of understanding human
cognitive powers. His work, highly schematic and typo-
logical, is based on an inadequate basis of information.
This means that he is tempted to brandish his grand
generalizations prematurely. Lévi-Strauss never leaves
any mystery unsolved. His method for analyzing complex
structures of contrast and similarity applies to anything
and everything. It never fails. A method adapted from

linguistic and literary analysis, it appears to be much more than a mere method, because its application to esoteric and ancient myths enters a claim to unveil the hidden movement of our prehistoric consciousness. Since it draws a special appeal from this claim to interpret primitive thought,[12] he keeps alive the practical dichotomy which assigns anthropology to the shallows and purlieus of philosophy.

To conclude this side of the comparison between his work and Evans-Pritchard's, it is important to recognize that his is a different program of inquiry from that which took its roots in William James's interest in mental associations, in Frederick Bartlett's concern with memory, and in Marcel Mauss's questions about the socializing of the physical body. The latter asked about how incoming sensory data are screened and organized, how memory functions, what selective principles of attention are at work, and which social factors enter into the cognitive process. Though Lévi-Strauss has offered some ideas on these topics,[13] they are not central to his main interests and influence.

These cursory remarks drawn in light and dark are intended to sharpen the contrast with Evans-Pritchard, to show up the strengths and weaknesses of each. The Englishman was wary of grand intellectual schemes, careful to a point of scrupulosity about correct translation. His strength was in fieldwork, his weakness in schematic ordering. This very weakness came from a personal skepticism about the possibility of objective knowledge and thence from an unusual sophistication on epistemological matters. By comparison, Lévi-Strauss often seems to walk in eighteenth-century innocence. For him data is data, however gathered: when he discovers error, he

[12] C. Lévi-Strauss, *La Pensée Sauvage* (*The Savage Mind*).
[13] Ibid.

corrects his theories and realigns his scheme, but his greatness in interpretative synthesis is not matched by sensitivity to problems about subjective awareness. So the two great contemporary anthropologists, with all due respect for each other, were following different lights, attracted to different problems, and working in different ways.

Evans-Pritchard's implicit conception of human knowledge starts from three principles. First, rational thought is exercised only selectively over the possible field of attention. Second, the principles of selectivity depend upon the social demand for accountability. Third, the social patterns of accountability which can be elicited by systematic observation provide a structured anchorage for a particular kind of reality, with its own array of beings invested with appropriate powers. In sum, each human society, insofar as its members expect to hold each other accountable, has its own locally selected reality anchored to agreement about moral objectives. Going beyond a literary and impressionistic stage of research, the anthropologist should

> discover the structural order of the society, so that it is intelligible not merely at the level of consciousness and action, as it is to one of its members or to the foreigner who has learnt its mores and participated in its life, but also at the level of sociological analysis. Just as the linguist does not merely seek to understand, speak and translate a native language but seeks to reveal its phonological and grammatical systems, so the social anthropologist is not content merely to observe and describe the social life of a primitive people but seeks to reveal its underlying structural order, the patterns which, once established, enable him to see it as a whole, as a set of interrelated abstractions.[14]

[14] *Social Anthropology* (Broadcast Lectures), pp. 61–62.

Having identified these structural patterns in one society, the social anthropologist is expected to compare
them with patterns in other societies. I said above that
Evans-Pritchard was guided by a feeling for epistemological directness. When he wrote about beliefs and meanings he assumed straightforwardly that a statement
would only be counted as a belief if actions were consistently observed to be consistent with its truth. His
teaching implied that a consensual commitment to a way
of life is inherently a commitment to a way of thought
and vice versa. Michael Polanyi,[15] who was much influenced by Evans-Pritchard's Azande study, was one
of the few in England at that time to be interested
in what he called the fiduciary element, or the element
of commitment and trust, in any knowledge. Now that
the air has cleared and now that philosophers have
worked through the pitfalls of earlier controversies,
Evans-Pritchard emerges from the past as if he had,
impossibly, been reared in a modern theory of knowledge.
I would say not that he was saved by luck, or made
modern by the turn of the wheel, but that he was legiti-
mately ahead of the game because of a powerful insight
and patient reasoning.

He had worked out how to relate sentences to beliefs
with maximum confidence, by checking to see how much
the speakers staked upon what they said. From this
securer basis in comparative accountability, we note that
different accounting systems would call forth different
arrays of hard physical facts. By emphasizing this use of
accountability as a common area of human experience
on which to base common understanding and safer
interpretation, I exaggerate any claim to a special methodology he would have been prepared to make. Evans-

[15] M. Polanyi, *Personal Knowledge*, pp. 287–94.

Pritchard was not too modest to claim methodological insights. He was too skeptical at too fundamental a personal level to seek or claim security in knowledge. He did not think the problems are easy or that any guarantees of truth can be trusted.

> We feel like spectators at a shadow show watching insubstantial shadows on the screen. There is nothing Nuer can say of the nature of God or other spirits than that he is like the wind or air. . . .[16]

> A study of the symbols tells us nothing of the nature of what is symbolized. Spirit in itself is for the Nuer a mystery which lies behind the names and the totemic and other appearances in which it is represented. . . .

> Words and gestures transport us to a realm of experience when what the eye sees and the ear hears is not the same as what the mind perceives. Hands are raised in supplication to the sky, but the sky is not being supplicated.[17]

The ancestor's antique spear is really a new spear recently bought from an Arab trader. Or the ancestral spear is nonexistent, a man making gestures with it by moving his empty hand as if the spear were there. The sacrificial ox stands for the sacrifice, but the sacrificer may not be present at all; even the ox may be represented by a cucumber.

> We seem indeed to be watching a play or to be listening to someone's account of what he has dreamt. Perhaps when we have this illusion we are beginning to understand, for the significance of the objects, actions and events lies not in themselves, but in what they mean to those who experience them as participants or assistants. . . . when we reflect on their meaning we per-

[16] *Nuer Religion*, p. 321.
[17] Ibid.

ceive they are a dramatic representation of a spiritual experience.[18]

Given this profound philosophical doubt and given that his ways of dealing with it were provisional suspensions or containments, what right have I to claim that his attention to misfortune is a methodologically central tool? None, no right, but I have good reasons for drawing attention to the resounding implications of his usage. At this time, younger anthropologists, beset by philosophical quandaries from which they see no escape, are content to treat the best understanding they can report as well-observed, deeply interpreted fictional texts.[19] Evans-Pritchard's descriptions also probe contradictory statements and reveal the delicate strain and balance between desires. For such penetrating sensitivity he was once described as the Stendhal of anthropology. But he showed the way to do something different from fiction. By systematically attending to people's response to misfortune, he justified the distinctive claims of his chosen profession.

[18] *Nuer Religion*, p. 322.
[19] C. Geertz, "Found in Translation: On the Social History of the Modern Imagination."

SHORT BIBLIOGRAPHY

WORKS BY EVANS-PRITCHARD

"The Intellectualist (English) Interpretation of Magic," *Bulletin of the Faculty of Arts* (Egyptian University, Cairo) I (1933), pp. 282–311.

"Lévy-Bruhl's Theory of Primitive Mentality," *Bulletin of the Faculty of Arts* (Egyptian University) II (1934), pp. 1–36.

"Science and Sentiment: An Exposition and Criticism of the Writings of Pareto," *Bulletin of the Faculty of Arts* (Egyptian University), Part 2 (1936), pp. 163–92.

Witchcraft, Oracles, and Magic among the Azande. Oxford: The Clarendon Press, 1937.

"Some Aspects of Marriage and Family among the Nuer," *Zeitschrift für vergleichende Rechtswissenschaft* LII (1938), pp. 306–92.

The Nuer: A Description of the Modes of Livelihood and Political Institutions of a Nilotic People. Oxford: The Clarendon Press, 1940; New York: Oxford University Press, 1937.

"Social Anthropology: An Inaugural Address Delivered before the University of Oxford on 4 February 1948." Oxford: The Clarendon Press, 1948.

The Sanusi of Cyrenaica. New York: Oxford University Press, 1949.

"Social Anthropology: Past and Present" (The Marett Lecture), *Man* L, no. 198 (September 1950), pp. 118–24.

Kinship and Marriage among the Nuer. New York: Oxford University Press, 1951.

Social Anthropology (The Broadcast Lectures). London: Cohen and West, 1951.

Nuer Religion. New York: Oxford University Press, 1956.

Essays in Social Anthropology. London: Faber & Faber, 1962.

Theories of Primitive Religion. London and New York: Oxford University Press, 1965.

"Genesis of a Social Anthropologist," *The New Diffusionist* vol. 3, no. 10 (January 1973), pp. 17–23.

"Fragment of an Autobiography," *New Blackfriars* (January 1973), pp. 35–37.

WORKS BY OTHERS

Austin, J. L. *How to Do Things with Words.* Cambridge, Mass.: Harvard University Press, 1962.

Balfour, H. *Spinners and Weavers in Anthropological Research.* Oxford: The Clarendon Press, 1938.

Barnes, J. A. *Politics in a Changing Society.* Manchester: University of Manchester Press, 1967.

Bartlett, F. C. *Psychology and Primitive Culture.* Cambridge: Cambridge University Press, 1923.

————. *Remembering: A Study in Experimental and Social Psychology.* Cambridge: Cambridge University Press, 1932.

————. *Thinking: An Experimental and Social Study.* New York: Basic Books, 1958.

Bateson, G. *Naven* (second ed.). Palo Alto: Stanford University Press, 1958.

Bauman, Z. *Culture as Praxis.* London: Routledge & Kegan Paul, 1973.

Beattie, J., and Middleton, J., eds. *Spirit Mediumship and Society in Africa.* New York: Holmes & Meier, 1969.

Beidelman, T. O. "The Ox and Nuer Sacrifice: Some Freudian Hypotheses about Nuer Symbolism," *Man* I, no. 4 (1966), pp. 453–67.

————. "Some Nuer Notions of Nakedness, Nudity, and Sexuality," *Africa* XXXVIII, no. 2 (1968), pp. 113–32.

Boas, F. "The Study of Geography," in *Race, Language, and Culture.* New York: Macmillan, 1887.

Bohannon, L. "A Genealogical Charter," *Africa* XXII, no. 4 (1952).

Buxton, J. *Religion and Healing in Mandari.* New York: Oxford University Press, 1973.

Cicourel, A. *Cognitive Sociology.* New York: Free Press, 1973.

Colson, E. "Spirit Possession among the Tonga of Zambia," in Beattie and Middleton, eds., *Spirit Mediumship and Society in Africa.*

Crocker, J. C. "My Brother the Parrot," in Sapir, Crocker, and Christopher, eds., *The Social Use of Metaphor: Essays on the Anthropology of Rhetoric.* Philadelphia: University of Pennsylvania Press, 1977.

Cunnison, I. G. *The Luapula Peoples of Northern Rhodesia.* Atlantic Highlands, N.J.: Humanities Press, 1959.

Davis, J. *People of the Mediterranean.* London and Boston: Routledge & Kegan Paul, 1977.

Douglas, M., ed. *Witchcraft Accusations and Confessions.* London: Tavistock Publications, 1970.

Dumont, L. Preface to *Les Nuers.* Paris: Editions Gallimard (I–XV), 1968.

Ferrero, G. *Les Lois Symboliques du Symbolisme* (1895). Reference in Haddon, *Evolution in Art,* pp. 300–301.

Firth, R., ed. *Man and Culture: An Evaluation of the Work of Bronislaw Malinowski.* London and Boston: Routledge & Kegan Paul, 1957, 1970.

Fortes, M. *Oedipus and Job in West African Religion.* New York: Octagon Books, 1978.

―――. "Pietas in Ancestor Worship," *Journal of the Royal Anthropological Institute* XCI, no. 2 (1961), pp. 166–91.

―――. "La Notion de Personne en Afrique Noire," *Colloques Internationaux du Centre National de la Recherche Scientifique* 544 (1971), pp. 283–319.

―――. "Custom and Conscience in Anthropological Perspective," *International Review of Psychoanalysis* IV (1977), pp. 127–54.

Foucault, M. "L'Ordre du Discours," in *Archéologie du Savoir.* Paris: Gallimard, 1964.

Frazer, J. G. *The Golden Bough* (third ed.). New York: St. Martin's Press, 1936.

Fry, P. *Spirits of Protest.* Cambridge and New York: Cambridge University Press, 1976.

Geertz, C. "Religion as a Cultural System," in *Anthropological Approaches to the Study of Religion.* London: Tavistock Publications, 1966.

―――. *The Interpretation of Cultures.* New York: Basic Books, 1973.

―――. "Found in Translation: On the Social History of the Modern Imagination," *The Georgia Review* XXXI, no. 4 (1977), pp. 788–810.

Gellner, E. *Saints of the Atlas.* Chicago: University of Chicago Press, 1969.

Gombrich, E. H. *Art and Illusion* (paperback ed). Princeton: Princeton University Press, 1972.

Haddon, A. C. *The Decorative Art of New Guinea: A Study in Papuan Ethnography.* Royal Irish Academy Memoirs, 1894; New York: AMS Press, 1977.

———. *Evolution in Art as Illustrated by the Life Histories of Designs.* London, 1895; New York: AMS Press, 1976.

Halbwachs, M. *Les Cadres Sociaux de la Mémoire (The Social Framework of Memory).* Paris, 1925; New York: Arno Press, 1975.

———. "La Mémoire Collective chez les Musiciens," *Revue Philosophique* (1939), pp. 136–65.

———. *La Morphologie Sociale.* Paris, 1938.

———. *La Mémoire Collective (Collective Memory).* Paris: Presses Universitaires de France, 1950; New York: Harper & Row, 1978.

Horton, R. "Destiny and the Unconscious in West Africa," *Africa* XXXI, no. 2 (1967), pp. 110–16.

———. "African Traditional Thought and Western Science," *Africa* XXXVII, nos. 1 and 2 (1967), pp. 50–71; 155–87.

———. "Types of Spirit Possession in Kalabari Religion," in Beattie and Middleton, eds., *Spirit Mediumship and Society in Africa.*

———. "African Conversion," *Africa* XLI, no. 2 (1971), pp. 85–108.

———. "On the Rationality of Conversion," *Africa* XLV, nos. 3 and 4 (1975), pp. 219–35; 373–99.

Kuhn, T. S. *The Structure of Scientific Revolutions.* Chicago: University of Chicago Press, 1962.

Lang, A. *The Making of Religion* (second ed.). London: Longmans Green, 1900; reprint of 1898 edition, New York: AMS Press, 1979.

Leach, E. R. "The Epistemological Background to Malinowski's Empiricism," in Firth, ed., *Man and Culture,* pp. 119–37.

Lévi-Strauss, C. *La Pensée Sauvage (The Savage Mind).* Paris: Plon, 1962; Chicago: University of Chicago Press, 1966.

Lévy-Bruhl, L. "A Letter to E. E. Evans-Pritchard," *British Journal of Sociology* III, no. 2 (1952), pp. 117–23.

———. *How Natives Think.* New York: Washington Square Press, 1966. First ed., *Les Fonctions mentales dans les sociétés inférieures,* Paris, 1910.

Lewis, I. M. *A Pastoral Democracy.* London: Oxford University Press (for the International African Institute), 1961.

————. *Ecstatic Religion.* Harmondsworth and Baltimore: Penguin Books, 1971.

Lienhardt, G. *Divinity and Experience: The Religion of the Dinka.* New York: Oxford University Press, 1961.

————. "E. P.: A Personal View," *Man* (New Series) 9 (1974), pp. 299–304.

Lowie, R. *History of Ethnological Theory.* New York: Holt Rinehart & Winston, 1937.

Malinowski, B. *Coral Gardens and Their Magic,* II. 1935; New York: Dover Publications, 1978.

Marwick, M. G. *Sorcery in Its Social Setting: A Study of the North Rhodesian Cewa.* Baltimore: Penguin Books, 1970.

Mauss, M. "Les Téchniques du Corps," *Journal de Physiologie* 3–4 (1936); extract in *Sociologie et Anthropologie,* Paris: Presses Universitaires de France, 1936.

Merton, R. K. "Karl Mannheim and the Sociology of Knowledge," in *Social Theory and Social Structure* (enlarged ed.). New York: Free Press, 1941.

————. "The Sociology of Knowledge," in *Social Theory and Social Structure* (enlarged ed.). New York: Free Press, 1945.

Middleton, J. *Lugbara Religion.* London: Oxford University Press (for the International African Institute), 1960.

Middleton, J., and Winter, E. H., eds. *Witchcraft and Sorcery in East Africa.* London: Routledge & Kegan Paul, 1963.

Mitchell, J. C. *The Yao Village.* Manchester: Manchester University Press, 1956; Atlantic Highlands, N.J.: Humanities Press, 1971.

Murphy, R. F. "Tuary Kinship," *American Anthropologist* 69 (1967), pp. 167–70.

Nadel, S. F. "Malinowski on Magic and Religion," in Firth, ed., *Man and Culture.*

Nygren, A. *Agape and Eros.* New York: Harper & Row, 1969; originally *Eros och Agape,* Stockholm, 1936.

Otto, R. *Das Heilige (The Idea of the Holy).* London: Oxford University Press, 1923; second ed., New York: Oxford University Press, 1958.

Percy, W. "The Symbolic Structure of Interpersonal Process," *Psychiatry* 24 (1961), pp. 39–52.

Peristiany, J. G. *Honour and Shame: The Values of Mediterranean Society.* Chicago: University of Chicago Press, 1974.

Peters, E. L. "The Proliferation of Segments in the Lineage of the Bedouin of Cyrenaica," *Journal of the Royal Anthropo-*

logical Institute of Great Britain and Ireland 90 (1960), pp. 29–53.

Pitkin, H. F. *Wittgenstein and Justice.* Berkeley: University of California Press, 1973.

Pitt-Rivers, J. *The People of the Sierra.* Chicago: University of Chicago Press, 1961.

Polanyi, M. *Personal Knowledge.* London: Routledge & Kegan Paul, 1973; Chicago: University of Chicago Press, 1958.

Quine, W. V. *Word and Object.* Cambridge, Mass.: The MIT Press, 1960.

Radcliffe-Brown, A. R. *The Andaman Islanders.* Cambridge: Cambridge University Press, 1933.

Ray, B. C. *African Religions: Symbol, Ritual and Community.* Englewood Cliffs, N.J.: Prentice-Hall, 1976.

Rignano, E. *Psicologia del ragionamento (The Psychology of Reasoning).* Bologna: Zanichelli, 1920; New York: Harcourt Brace, and Co.

Salim, S. M. *Marsh Dwellers of the Euphrates Delta.* London: Athlone Press, 1962.

Schafer, R. *A New Language for Psychoanalysis.* New Haven: Yale University Press, 1976.

Schapera, I. *Rainmaking Rites of Tswana Tribes.* Cambridge: African Studies Center, 1971.

Seligman, C. G., and Seligman, B. *Pagan Tribes of the Nilotic Sudan.* London: G. Routledge & Son, 1932.

Sharpe, E. *Comparative Religion: A History.* London: Duckworth, 1975.

Sherrington, C. S. *Man on His Nature* (second ed.). New York: Cambridge University Press, 1953.

Singer, A., and Street, B. V., eds. *Zande Themes: Essays Presented to Sir Edward Evans-Pritchard.* Totowa, N.J.: Rowman and Littlefield, 1972.

Smith, G. Elliot. *In the Beginning: The Origin of Civilization.* New York: Morrow, 1928.

Smith, J. Z. "I Am a Parrot (Red)," *History of Religions* II (1972), pp. 391–413.

Smith, W. Robertson. *The Religion of the Semites: The Fundamental Institutions.* London: A. & C. Black, 1889; New York: Schocken Books, 1972.

Steinen, K. von den. *Unter der Naturvolken Zentral-Brasiliens.* Berlin, 1894; Chicago: Johnson, 1894.

Stirling, A. P. *Turkish Village.* London: Weidenfeld & Nicolson, 1965.

Thomas, K. "Should Historians Be Anthropologists?" *The Oxford Magazine* (1961), pp. 387–88.

Turner, V. W. *Schism and Continuity in an African Society: A Study of Ndembu Village Life*. Manchester: Manchester University Press, 1957; Atlantic Highlands, N.J.: Humanities Press, 1972.

Tyler, S. A. "Introduction," in Tyler, ed., *Cognitive Anthropology*. New York: Holt, Rinehart & Winston, 1969.

Van der Leeuw, G. *La Structure de la Mentalité Primitive*. Paris, 1928.

Vygotsky, L. *Thought and Language*. Cambridge: The MIT Press, 1962.

Wiener, N. *Cybernetics*. New York: John Wiley, 1948.

Winch, P. "Understanding a Primitive Society," *American Philosophical Quarterly* I (1964), pp 307-24

Wittgenstein, L. *Philosophical Investigations* (trans. G. E. M. Anscombe). Oxford: Basil Blackwell, 1972; New York: Macmillan, 1973.

Zaretsky, I. I., and Shambaugh, C., eds. *Spirit Possession and Spirit Mediumship in Africa and Afro-America: An Annotated Bibliography*. New York and London: Garland Publishing, 1978.

INDEX

Abstractions in philosophy, 33

Accountability, 2, 3, 31–33, 94, 111, 127, 132–34

Accountability among the Azande, 48–60; accusations, 50–52, 56–57; aristocrats and, 57; autopsy of convicted witches, 52; boundaries of system of, 56–57; changes under Anglo-Egyptian Condominium, 53–54; curiosity about "Why me?" question, 48–49; inheritance of witchcraft, 50, 52, 55–58; institutions and ideas, relationship between, 57–58; unconscious witchcraft, 50, 56; vengeance, 51, 53–54. *See also* Oracles, Azande

Accountability among the Nuer, 71–74, 82, 84–85; "being in the right," concept of, 103; religion and, 103–105, 107; spirits and God, 118

Adoption among Nuer, 80–81

Agape (agapo), 96; Christian concept of, 97–101, 105, 114

Anthropology (anthropologists): American, 126, 127; British, 127–29; Evans-Pritchard's influence on, 126–35; history and, 111, 112; in 1920s, 6–7; religion and, 110–13. *See also* Fieldwork; *and specific topics*

145